William Pittenger. Frontispiece from Daring and Suffering: A History of the Great Railroad Adventure. *1863.*

FOREWORD

William Pittenger was an American soldier, professor, minister, and elocutionist.

In 1895, not long after he left his teaching position at the American School of Elocution and Oratory in Philadelphia, he penned the book you hold in your hands: *Toasts and Forms of Public Address for Those Who Wish to Say the Right Thing in the Right Way.*

Despite the book's stature as one of the more important public speaking titles in its day, the book is overshadowed by other events in a remarkable life. Pittenger's legacy was not shaped by his ministry, his speech-writing, or his commitment to the flag—it was shaped by a silent film producer who was given a copy of his memoir years after Pittenger had passed.

EARLY LIFE

Born on January 31st, 1840 in Knoxville, Ohio, William Pittenger grew up on a farm. He was a sturdy child, but suffered from eyesight so bad that "when he began to read he could distinguish the letters of his book only at the distance of three inches; he never attempted to distinguish persons by the faces, but by the sound of their voices" (A Unique Story of the War, 1888).

William's father, Thomas, was eventually able to purchase eyeglasses when the boy reached fifteen years of age. When William first saw the stars in the sky, his life changed:

> With the naked eye he could see stars of not less than the third magnitude; but with his spectacles the magnificence of the starry heavens was revealed to him.

> "No language," he says, "can describe the glory of the heavens that burst on my view with all the

charm of novelty. I soon longed for the means to see more of the wonder of the stars. Having no money, and telescopes being costly, it was necessary to secure additional means (A Unique Story of the War, 1888).

It's hard to overstate the urgency with which William wanted to see the stars more closely. He needed money for a better telescope now. Teaching seemed to William the most surefire way to secure a wage and purchase a telescope, and so he applied for a teaching license before his 16th birthday. However, this profession was also out of his reach as someone with such poor eyesight, even with glasses:

The Board of Examiners of Jefferson County declared that while not disqualified, from a literary standpoint, I was too near-sighted to control a band of unruly children. They were more than half right. I was not then sixteen. A few months later I made another attempt, and as I had then become more accustomed to my glasses, which had been purchased just before the first examination, the certificate was granted (A Unique Story of the War, 1888).

William built a much more powerful telescope with his first paychecks, but was disappointed to discover that despite his enhanced equipment, his eyes still held him back. Though his peers could see new details clearly, Pittinger's eyes were barely able to see the difference: "I required twice as much instrumental power for the purpose as my visitors, [preventing] me from becoming a professional astronomer" (A Unique Story of the War, 18888).

William continued his studies in astronomy while he taught Knoxville's youth. This would be interrupted in a few years, however, as war was about to divide the country.

CIVIL WAR

"A bookish fellow with glasses [and] the temperament of a preacher," Pittenger "almost didn't make it into the Army because he couldn't see what he was doing" (Cannon, 2016).

At the start of the war, in April of 1861, President Lincoln called for 90-day enlistments, allowing citizens to serve their country on a short-term basis as the Union was hopeful for a quick resolution. Raised in a devoutly religious household, Pittenger saw the war as an opportunity to help eradicate the practice of slavery. In Reverend Alexander Clark's introduction to Pittenger's account of the war, *Daring and Suffering*, he describes the author:

> Any mind imbued with an admiration of God's marches in the Heavens as an Omnipotent Creator, and inspired by a contemplation of God's finger in History as a merciful Deliverer, will rise to the high level of universal love to man, and will comprehend the broad equality of Gospel liberty and republican brotherhood...

> When Pittenger became a volunteer, it was for the suppression of the Rebellion with all its belongings— and if its overthrow should tumble

slavery, with its clanking fetters and howling hounds, to the uttermost destruction, he would grasp his gun the firmer for the hope, and thank God for the prospect, the test, and the toil! He enlisted as a soldier for his country, ready to march anywhere, strike with any weapon, endure any fatigue, or share any sorrow. He went out not merely an armored warrior, to ward off attacks, not to strike off obnoxious top-growths; but to "lay the ax at the root of the tree," and to pierce the very heart of the monster iniquity (Pittenger, Daring and Suffering: A History of the Great Railroad Adventure, 1863).

Though written in retrospect, it seemed clear to those who knew him that William Pittenger was destined to serve.

Despite his near-sightedness, he managed to enlist in the Union army as a private, and began his service in the 2nd Ohio Infantry Regiment's "H" Company.

I did not vote for Lincoln for president, only because I lacked a few months of twenty-one. But I exerted all my influence in that direction; and when predictions of war were made if he should be elected, I did not deny the probability, but maintained that the war would be short, leading directly to the abolition of slavery, and professed a willingness to enlist for the purpose of putting down that institution with the rebellion. When I wrote home, saying that in the event of a war I had made up my mind to become a soldier, my father gave his consent very readily; his reasons, as he afterwards explained, being that he did not believe that there would be any war; and if there was, he felt sure that I would not, because of bad sight, be accepted as a soldier (A Unique Story of the War, 1888).

William's first posting was in Washington, DC to help protect the capitol from the Confederates' possible approach—but that quiet posting soon brought him to the forefront of the war, when troops were spotted thirty miles from the capitol (Wintermantel, 2014). This was the bloody First Battle of Bull Run, where, in July 1861, tens of thousands of troops on both sides suffered tremendous losses. The Union lost almost ten percent of its soldiers at that engagement, and the Confederacy lost around seven percent of its combatants. It was a Confederate victory that made the country realize that this would not be a short conflict (Encyclopedia Britannica, 2023).

In Pittenger's report to the Stubenville Weekly Herald, for whom he had volunteered as a war correspondent, he shares the horror:

> The whistling of the bullets was more loud than pleasant, and in surprise many dodged from the ranks into the bushes, but soon returned to their places... Meanwhile, the shot was flying thick around, crashing through the trees in every direction. Every little while we could hear the scream of a wounded man, as the balls struck him. One poor fellow who was lying not far from me, was torn to pieces by a shot. The bombs, of which only a few were thrown, were the most destructive...

(Pittenger, Army Correspondence, 1861).

This experience bolstered Pittenger's resolve. He signed up for a three-year service once his 90-day enlistment had finished, taking a scant few days at home to rest (Pittenger, Daring and Suffering: A History of the Great Railroad Adventure, 1863). He was sent to Camp Dennison in Ohio and quickly promoted to sergeant in 1862. Soon, he would volunteer to take part in an adventure that would become a focal point of his life—and would result in one of the most celebrated silent movies of all time.

THE GREAT LOCOMOTIVE CHASE

"Andrews Raid" was a secret mission planned by the Union Army. Soldiers, led by the spy James J. Andrews, were going to capture a Confederate train in Marietta, Georgia. Once onboard, they would lay waste to every bridge and telegraph line between that town and Chattanooga, Tennessee. Pittenger tells the story:

> "Boys," [Andrews] said, "we are entering on a very hazardous expedition, but it will be a glorious one in its results, and will give the enemy the most deadly blow he has

yet received. What a grand thing it will be to run through the South, leaving the bridges burning, and the foe in helpless rage behind! If we burn those bridges, Mitchel will capture Chattanooga the very next day, and all of East Tennessee will be open before him. But we must be prompt, for if he gets to Huntsville before us, the road will be so crowded with reinforcements moving against him that our task will be much harder. But if we have the bridges down first, they can send no force against him, and he will have everything his own way. The last train leaves Chattanooga for Marietta at five in the afternoon.

Be sure to catch it not later than Thursday, and I will either be on it or on an earlier one—Good-bye!"

...

The group went to Georgia with the cover story of being rebels from Kentucky who wanted to escape "Yankee rule". They managed to take over the train [*The General*] without any issue whatsoever, but then... the train pulled to a halt... When the train halted at Big Shanty the dampers of the engine furnace had been closed; they had not been opened when the start was made, and the fire was almost out. They had been running by the steam stored up in the boilers, which was

Participants the Great Locomotive Chase of the American Civil War. Seven of the raiders (James J. Andrews, William Campbell, Samuel Llewellyn, Samuel Robertson, Perry Shadrack, James Smith, George D. Wilson) are not pictured.

1. *Mark Wood, Private, Company C, 21st Ohio Infantry*
2. *William J. Knight, Private, Company E, 21st Ohio Infantry*
3. *Daniel A. Dorsey, Corporal, Company H, 33rd Ohio Infantry*
4. *Robert Buffum, Private, Company H, 21st Ohio Infantry*
5. *John A. Wilson, Private, Company C, 21st Ohio Infantry*
6. *William Bensinger, Private, Company G, 21st Ohio Infantry*
7. *William Reddick, Corporal, Company B, 33rd Ohio Infantry*
8. *John Wollam, Private, Company C, 33rd Ohio Infantry*

now exhausted. But fresh wood and a little oil put matters to rights, and they were soon underway, with time enough to attend to obstructing the track behind them and to cut the telegraph-wire. When they were fairly on their way again, Andrews broke out into a joyful shout: "We have got them at such a disadvantage that they cannot harm us or save

---

9. *William A. Fuller, train conductor who chased the raiders*
10. *Wilson W. Brown, Private, Company F, 21st Ohio Infantry*
11. *Samuel Slavens, Private, Company E, 33rd Ohio Infantry*
12. *Elihu H. Mason, Sergeant, Company K, 21st Ohio Infantry*
13. *Martin J. Hawkins, Corporal, Company A, 33rd Ohio Infantry*
4. *Marian (or Marion) A. Ross, Sergeant Major, 2nd Ohio Infantry*
15. *John R. Porter, Private, Company G, 21st Ohio Infantry*
16. *Jacob Parrott, Private, Company K, 33rd Ohio Infantry*
17. *John M. Scott, Sergeant, Company F, 21st Ohio Infantry*
18. *Andrew Murphy, train machinist who chased the raiders*
19. *William Pittinger, Sergeant Major, 21st Ohio Infantry*
From Deeds of Valor, Vol. 1. *1907.*

themselves. When we have passed one more train, we'll have no further hindrance; then we'll put the engine at full speed, burn the bridges after us, dash through Chattanooga, and on to Mitchel at Huntsville. We have the upper hand of the rebels for once!"

Unfortunately for the raiders, heavy rains made the bridges difficult to burn. The track they damaged halted their pursuers, who had to continue their chase on foot. Once past the broken tracks the Confederates encountered a southbound train, The Texas. Putting the engine in reverse, they picked up a group of soldiers armed with rifles, and sped backwards at an almost unheard-of velocity of 60 miles per hour in pursuit of *The General* (Military Heroes, 2022).

Andrews and his raiders were in trouble.

> [*The General* and its commandeers] eventually run out of fuel, and are caught by a locomotive in hot pursuit—driven by the very engineer they had just removed from *The General*:

> "They had indeed made their last throw, and lost. The smoke of the pursuing engine[1] was seen close at hand. The enemy had the advantage of being armed with guns, and

would be able to fire upon them at long range, while they only had their revolvers. The coupling-pin was withdrawn, and the slowly-burning car was detached from the engine. The pursuers dashed into the thick smoke that filled the covered bridge, and pushed the burning car on to Ringgold, but a short distance ahead, where it was left to smoke and sputter in the rain on the side track. *The General* crept slowly on until about five miles beyond Ringgold—some twenty miles below Chattanooga. But the fuel was utterly exhausted."
(A Unique Story of the War, 1888)

The General is abandoned by the raiders. From Battles and Leaders of the Civil War. *1887.*

Despite their success in capturing *The General*, Andrews and his band of saboteurs were plagued with bad luck—it was impossible for them to account for other trains on the tracks, and were quickly chased down by The Texas. Their mission was a failure, having destroyed one train track and cut a single telegraph cable. The raid was finished, having failed to cripple the Confederacy's most important transportation and communication infrastructure. Some soldiers managed to escape into the woods, but their freedom didn't last long—the entire band had been captured within two weeks.

CAPTURE & ACCLAIM

The raiders were tried in Confederate military courts and found guilty of "acts of unlawful belligerency." Andrews, the ringleader, was hanged, as were seven others who were transferred from Georgia to a prison camp in Knoxville. Fearing the same fate, Parrott and the remaining raiders made their escape. Eight succeeded, but Parrott and five others were caught in the attempt. Held again as a prisoner of war, Parrott was beaten more than 100 times in an effort to get him to divulge more about the raiders' intentions.

At the Prisoner of War Camp in Lafayette, Georgia, a Methodist minister befriended Pittenger, lending him books to read, furthering his religious transformation: "I did not care [for law books] but the fact that many, though not all, of the minister's books were of the theological and religious cast only made them more welcome. This Atlanta jail was my seminary...." Pettinger and others were eventually released in a prisoner exchange. In a poetic book-end to the affair, Pittenger took the train home and was greeted by relatives at Sloane's Station, near his hometown in Ohio.

"The journey over the old familiar hills about which I had dreamed in Southern dungeons," he wrote, "the tearful welcome of father and mother, the surprise and joy of the little brother and sisters. For the first time in history a public supper was given in honor of an individual in the little village of Knoxville.[1] The next Sunday I

---

1 Today, a historical marker celebrates Pittenger's story in Knoxville, Ohio. (The Historical Marker Database, 2020).

attended the Methodist church in New Somerset and had my name enrolled as a probationer. The vow I had made to God in hour of trouble was not forgotten" (The Victoria Warder, 1888).

MEDAL OF HONOR

On March 6th, 1863, Parrott, Pittenger, and the other four surviving raiders were awarded a newly approved medal for valor. The cohort, however, had notable absences: Andrews (who was executed immediately after his trial at the POW camp) and Campbell (who miraculously survived). As civilians, these two were not eligible for any such commendation (Gindlesperger, 2022).

It wasn't just any award. The award they received was the newly-minted Congressional Medal of Honor.

Pittenger was the fifth to receive the prize that day[2] (Military Aviation Preservation Society (MAPS), 2022)—his colleague, Parrot, was the first to receive the award on account of the brutal torture he

---

2   Interestingly, Pittenger's personal diary from 1863 has no entries between March 5th and 11th, 1863, when the ceremonies surrounding the Medal of Honor took place. An entry on the 4th simply reads "Smallpox." An entry on the 12th Mentions the passing of sergeant E. J. Reynolds at a hospital in Memphis "with the long fever," closing with "peace to his ashes" (Pittenger, Civil War Diaries, 2023).

endured at the hands of Confederate soldiers, desperate to learn more about the raiders and their secret plans (Gindlesperger, 2022).

In his memoirs, Pittenger reflected on the presentation:

> Secretary Stanton next presented us one hundred dollars each from the secret service fund as pocket money, and gave orders for payment to us of all arrearages, and for refunding the full value of the money and arms taken from us at our capture... We were then escorted to the executive mansion and had a most pleasing

interview with President Lincoln (Cannon, 2016).

However, as the war raged on, he also lamented:

> But the end was not yet. The rebel leaders, who had embarked their all in this cause, and had pictured to themselves a magnificent slaveholding empire, stretching away from the Potomac to the Sierra Madre, in Mexico, and swallowing up all tropical America in one mighty nation, devoted to the interests of cotton and slavery alone, over which they should reign, were not yet satisfied to relinquish their

cause as desperate, and abandon their glorious dreams. (Pittenger, Daring and Suffering: A History of the Great Railroad Adventure, 1863).

After receiving the commendation, with his enlistment over, William left the military. His official Medal of Honor citation reads:

One of the 19 of 22 men (including 2 civilians) who, by direction of Gen. Mitchell (or Buell), penetrated nearly 200 miles south into enemy territory and captured a railroad train at Big Shanty, Ga., in an attempt to destroy the bridges and

tract between Chattanooga and
Atlanta.

ACCREDITED TO:
STEUBENVILLE, JEFFERSON
COUNTY, OHIO
AWARDED POSTHUMOUSLY:
NO
PRESENTATION DATE &
DETAILS: MARCH 25, 1863
WASHINGTON, D.C.,
PRESENTED BY SEC. OF WAR
EDWARD M. STANTON

BORN: JANUARY 31, 1840,
KNOXVILLE, JEFFERSON
COUNTY, OH, UNITED
STATES

DIED: APRIL 24, 1904,
FALLBROOK, CA, UNITED
STATES
BURIED: ODD FELLOW
CEMETERY (MH),
FALLBROOK, CA, UNITED
STATES

(Congressional Medal of Honor
Society, 2022)

ORATORY

*Good-humor and brevity, an outline
and a story—what more is needed,
unless it be that serene self-confidence
which enables a speaker to say even
foolish and absurd things, with the*

assurance that all goes down at a
public dinner?

– William Pittenger

(Pittenger, *Toasts and Forms of Public Address for Those Who Wish to Say the Right Thing in the Right Way*, 1895).

When William Pittenger left the army, he became a minister. Having rekindled his devotion to God in that Confederate prison, he joined the Pittsburgh conference of the Methodist Episcopal Church in 1864 (Young, 2018). He was sent to preach in New Jersey in 1870, and worked as a pastor there for almost two decades.

At this time, Pittenger also began working at the National School of Elocution and Oratory.[3] This was a new school, only five years old, across the river in Philadelphia.

Its founders, Jacob and Rachel H. Shoemaker, had worked as instructors at a variety of schools—public, private, and for freedmen—where Jacob recognized that "a lucid method of expression aided his pupils' comprehension of whatever

3   The National School of Elocution and Oratory no longer stands today. It was located at 1418 Chestnut Street in Philadelphia, Pennsylvania (Philadelphia Architects and Buildings, 1880) (New England Journal of Education, 1880).

subjects he presented and how much the proper vocalization of his teachings went to impress them on the minds that he addressed. He therefore gave himself increasingly to the study of the principles of rhetoric and elocution, taught these extensively in the institutes throughout the State, and from 1866 labored in Philadelphia to build up a school that should embody and present these principles with full effect." William Pittenger would have been a perfect fit for them—a well-read preacher with a journalistic background and captivating stories to tell.

The school's 1874 catalogue showed an enrollment of 88 students during its second year of operation. The student body grew over the years, and survived the passing of its founders in 1880. In its first six years, the National School of Elocution and Oratory awarded more than 3,000 young elocutionists with Bachelor's and Master's degrees (Office of the Commissioner of Education, 1882).

It was renamed the "Shoemaker School of Speech and Drama" by the founders' daughter who took over as principal in 1915. The school closed its doors in the late 1930s, with a curriculum that included trends in journalism and radio technique (Philadelphia Inquirer, 1938).

By this time, however, Pittenger was long gone.

Pittenger was a strict teacher who demanded hard work from his students. In his book Extempore Speech he explains: "There is no trick in true oratory—no secret magic by which a weak-minded man can become the leader of other stronger and wiser than himself. The great prizes of eloquence cannot be placed in the hands of the ignorant or slothful. But so surely as a raw apprentice can be transformed into a skillful workman, any person possessed of ordinary faculties, who will pay the price in labor, can be made a master of the art of ready and forcible public utterance"

xlii

(Pittenger, Extempore Speech: and how to acquire and practice it, 1883).

William left Philadelphia and the National School of Elocution and Oratory in 1890. He moved his family to Fallbrook, California to minister at the small Episcopalian church there. Wherever he went, though, the Great Locomotive Chase seemed to follow him.

Soon after his move, Pittenger was invited to Chattanooga, Tennessee to deliver the closing prayer and unveiling ceremony of a monument dedicated to the fallen Andrews' Raiders. He continued to give lectures on the chase, spirituality, and the hardships he and his comrades endured during his nearly-year-long internment in Confederate POW camps. Alongside his ministry, Pittenger also remained deeply committed to education. He helped found Fallbrook's public school district and served as president of the school board there (Rivers, Pittenger Farm House, 1998).

Pittenger also staunchly defended the Union Army and the Congressional Medal of Honor whenever it was questioned in his circles. In an 1898 letter to the editor of The Christian Advocate, for example, he penned the following:

In the leading editorial of Oct. 27 the assertion is made that "in this country no such mark of distinction or appreciation" as the Victoria Cross "is conferred upon those sons of the republic who have made the story of our national life thrilling and glorious." Possibly our people care little for such decorations, or it may be that republics cannot make insignia of merit as splendid and valued as those bestowed by the head of a monarchy. But when the "medal of honor of the United States army" was handed to me by the Secretary of War in person, it was accompanied by the statement that this was the American equivalent of the Victoria

Cross and the French Cross of the Legion of Honor. Since then several hundred medals of honor have been given "for valor," and it is only to be regretted that greater popular recognition has not been accorded to the efforts of the government in this direction. I have now in hand a quarto volume given to each holder of the United States medal, and containing a most brilliant record of daring deeds. The first medals were given to six of the "Andrews Railroad Raiders" in April, 1863, and they have been continuously, though sparingly, issued to those thought worthy ever since.

-     William Pittenger, Fallbrook,

Cal.

(The Christian Advocate, 1898)

William Pittenger died in 1904 at the age of 64, and was buried at the Odd Fellows Cemetery in Fallbrook. A Medal of Honor marker was placed on his grave in 1988, over a century after it was awarded to him. His legacy, however, was firmly cemented in American history about two decades after his death—thanks to the silent comedian Buster Keaton.

BUSTER KEATON & *THE GENERAL*

In the early 1920s, Clyde Bruckman gave a copy of Pittenger's *Daring and Suffering: A History of the Great Railroad Adventure* to his friend and colleague, Buster Keaton (Stevens, 2022). Keaton was immediately taken with it. This book laid the foundations for one of the most lauded movies of the silent film age (and one of Buster Keaton's personal favorite projects)—*The General*.[4]

4   Interestingly, this was not the first film made about the Andrews' Raid. In 1911, Canadian film direct Sidney Olcott produced the film *The Railroad Raiders of '62* which portrays the events in under ten minutes (Olcott, 1911). Keaton's film was the first feature-length version of the story, and the only

Today, *The General* is considered one of the greatest American films ever made. However, when it was released in 1926, it was considered an absolute failure, both critically and commercially. The stunts in *The General* are some of the most dangerous in any Keaton film, featuring leaps from one train car to another, running along the rooftops of train cars, balancing on the moving train's cow-catcher, and obliviously sitting on the wheel's main rod as the locomotive starts moving (Neibaur, 2010). Keaton actually learned how to operate a steam engine for the sake of this film, underscoring his

---

one that doesn't take the events seriously.

dedication to performing his own stunts[5] (Axmaker, 2014).

The General cost over $750,000 in today's dollars to make, with the lion's share of that money being dedicated to a single shot. The climactic train crash and building of a 215-foot-long trestle bridge (built solely so it could be destroyed on camera) represented well over half of the budget. According to silent film historian Dana Stevens, "that fifteen-second-long take of a locomotive falling

---

5   Buster Keaton famously performed all of his own stunts, save one. In Keaton's 1927 film which followed *The General*, titled *College*, Olympic gold-medalist pole vaulter Lee Barnes replaced Keaton for a single shot (Stevens, 2022).

through a burning bridge into a river[6] was probably the most expensive single shot in silent film history" (Stevens, 2022). The box-office barely began to recoup the film's expenses, making approximately $475,000 across its release in today's dollars.

One of the most remarkable things about *The General* is how true to Pittenger's account—and, indeed, the rest of the Civil War—it stays. In an interview later in his life, Keaton is asked about a scene featuring a train-mounted cannon:

6   Roger Ebert claims that the rusting hulk of the locomotive used in filming is still at the bottom of the river to this day (Ebert, 1997), but other sources say it was hauled for scrap during World War II (Axmaker, 2014).

How did the [mounted] cannon sequence develop?

We found that. It's an actual gun of the Civil War. The first railroad gun. And we duplicated that cannon. It almost looks like a prop we invented. That's the only thing that kind of scared us. When it comes to using it. They said, "everybody's going to say, 'oh, they invented the prop just to get a gag'" but it's an actual reproduction of a railroad gun built in the Civil War... we found it in more than one book (Sweeney, 2007).

Keaton, Bruckman, and the rest of the team pored over Matthew Brady's famous photographs of the Civil War, ensuring that their costumes, sets, props, and other details were as true-to-life as possible. They got it so close, in fact, that stills of *The General* have been mistaken for Brady photographs by Civil War historians (Stevens, 2022). Using these photographs, Keaton "had modifications made to railway stock and passenger cars, created nineteenth-century building facades, and had costumes made when he could not secure actual Civil War-era materials. He grew out his hair to a length popular among Confederate soldiers, made his own hats, and ensured that co-star Marion Mack was dressed and groomed as a Southern woman of her station appeared in photographs." Keaton also set up his shots to mimic the still images taken by [Brady, Gardner, and other photographers] and their teams of war photographers" (Leonard, 2021). Comparing this to Disney's 1950s film based on Pittenger's story, one feels like a Hollywood pageant, the other a documentary.

The story was somewhat stripped down and streamlined, but followed Pittenger's account. The story was split into two chases that mirrored one another (racing North to re-capture the engine, then driving back South with the apprehended locomotive), adding liv a kidnapping and a love interest to give more sympathy to its hero. The piano music which accompanied the film was clearly designed to draw a Southern nostalgia from its audience, including variations on "Dixie" and other tunes connected with the American South (Leonard, 2021).

In the film, Buster portrays "Johnnie Gray," a Southern train conductor with two loves in his life—his girlfriend Annabelle Lee and his locomotive. When the train is stolen with his beau on board, Keaton desperately works to recapture the machine, ultimately apprehending it after chases on foot, bicycle, and handcar–chasing it down with another locomotive, The Texas. In the film, it's Keaton—not the raiders—who emerges victorious, with Buster almost single-handedly thwarting their attack.

When Keaton announced the new project, the owners of the original General refused to let him use the train. When they realized it was going to be a comedy (Leonard, 2021), they let Keaton know it was being restored for inclusion in the railroad museum at Kennesaw, Georgia.[7] He decided to move the filming from Georgia, where the events actually transpired, to Cottage Grove, Oregon,

---

7   Keaton was able, however, able to secure *The General*'s bell as a lobby display for the movie's premiere (Meade, 1997).

where there were plenty of railways, bridges, and scenery that would make the story sing (Giddins, 2008). He brought thousands of uniforms, two locomotives, and original Civil War artillery with him, hiring hundreds of Cottage Grove locals to fill in as extras (Axmaker, 2014).

Despite its lackluster reception at the time (newspapers described the locomotive as "a really great actor," told Buster to "pull it together. That's all," marveled at the sheer amount of money spent on the project ("no one denies the expenditure of a great deal of money,"), and rarely talked about the merits of the project itself,) it remained one of Buster's favorite projects (Stevens, 2022). He set out on the project with "ambition to make a really big comedy with a historical atmosphere... while this picture [was] designed primarily for laughs, it [was] my aim to make it historically correct and equally acceptable in the North and the South. It [was not] a burlesque, but a comedy spectacle of certain thrilling episodes in the struggle between the States" (Motion Picture News, 1926).

Keaton's desire to sell the movie on both sides of the Mason-Dixon Line is easy to see. The movie has a hapless Southern train conductor as its protagonist, allowing an audience to root for the underdog. It is essentially apolitical, containing no explicit references to slavery other than two men carrying a trunk—clearly coded as slaves—in the first five minutes, then never seen again. So keen was he to avoid a partisan response, the film premiered in Tokyo rather than the United States, to gauge the public's response (Leonard, 2021).

"I was more proud of that picture than any I ever made. Because I took an actual happening out of the... history books, and I told the story in detail too," said Keaton in a 1963 interview (Meade, 1997). And today, critics agree.

Buster Keaton cemented William Pittenger's legacy—along with that of the Andrews' Raiders—with his silent film send-up of the events, told from the Confederates' point of view.

And, though the movie doesn't rely on a single spoken word, it's every bit as eloquent in its storytelling as Pittenger would have demanded of his students.

WHAT MAKES THIS BOOK INTERESTING?

Pittenger's Toasts and Forms of Public Address for Those Who Wish to Say the Right Thing in the Right Way is interesting because it is not a book about etiquette.

At the turn of the century, there were a great number of books on toasting written as roadmaps for social mobility. The risks were great when giving a short speech as an aspiring member of the middle class—a misstep, an erroneous sentiment, or any signal of a less-than-lettered upbringing could mar your social standing. As such, most "toasting manuals" of the time are prescriptive in their approach. (In fact, the series of toasting books *Up-To-Date Toasts* by the Mutual Book Company of Boston, published in 1903, insists that their material should be memorized verbatim so as to ensure no missteps— but offers no guidance on how its lines should be recited!) As a result, many of these etiquette books are remarkably conservative in their tone, including commonly-held jingoistic, misogynistic, and racist sentiments along with lines about romance and love.

This book, however, is different in that it does not come from the etiquette tradition, and does not sell its contents as a "magic bullet" for social elevation. It's not about what to say, it's about how to say what you want to say. Pittenger's book comes from the tradition of elocution as a serious form of study, a self-described "science" that placed value on informing and inspiring an audience through oratory, stage presence, and gesture. If etiquette manuals taught their readers to fit in with the status quo, elocution books taught their readers to change minds and shape the world they wanted to see. It should come as no surprise, then, that this time period saw the rise of the American dime museum, the Chautauqua, and a reemergence the Lyceum circuit—all venues that needed professional lecturers to engage audiences hungry for information during a groundswell of civic awareness, temperance, spiritualism, abolition, and suffragette activism (Duchan, 2023).

Chautauqua, for example, was a traveling program that included music, variety entertainment, and public speaking. "The backbone of Chautauqua was the lecture," reminds professor emeritus Judith Duchan of The University of Buffalo's Department of Communicative Disorders and Sciences, "Religion, temperance, and politics proved to be the most popular subjects. Before radio became a valuable campaign tool, politicians found touring with circuit Chautauqua a useful way to gain national exposure... In the early years of this century, the Progressive Movement owed much of its success to the forums provided by Chautauqua" (Duchan, 2023). Dime museums and other venues also invited elocutionists to their stages to speak on a variety of topics, though usually on a non-touring model.

The concepts in this book show how professional speakers of the day understood their craft. "While recognizing the value of Rhetoric and Elocution," says James Bashford in his 1893 book *Practical Elements of Elocution*, "we must admit that they are only a means to an end. The aim of public speech is to influence hearers through the truth presented to them... for the sake of his hearers and for his own reputation, the speaker must be even more interested in finding the truth than in persuading the audience to accept the view he holds" (Cohen, 1995).

This book's value lies in its lessons. The turn of the century was a golden age of sorts for public speaking, a time before mass media and public broadcasts. The lessons here give a practical look at the tools used by masters of the craft. It is our hope that the republishing of this book helps others find their voice and engage audiences of their own.

BIBLIOGRAPHY

A Unique Story of the War. (1888, 9 8). *Literature: An Illustrated Weekly Magazine,* pp. 285-304.

Axmaker, S. (2014). The General. Retrieved October 15, 2023, from *San Francisco Silent Film Festival:* https://silentfilm.org/the-general/

Cannon, J. (2016, May 26). Union soldier survived a year in Confederate prison. Retrieved from *San Diego Union-Tribune:* https://www.sandiegouniontribune.com/military/sdut-union-soldier-survived-year-in-confederate-prison-2016may26-story.html

Cohen, H. (1995). The History of Speech Communication: The Emergence of a Discipline, 1914-1945. Washington, DC: National Communication Association.

Congressional Medal of Honor Society. (2022, 3 25). U.S. Civil War - U.S. Army. Retrieved from William PIttinger: https://www.cmohs.org/recipients/william-pittinger

Duchan, J. (2023, May 29). A History of Speech - Language Pathology: The Elocution Movement. Retrieved October 16, 2023,

from Judy Duchan - University of Buffalo:
https://www.acsu.buffalo.edu/~duchan/
new_history/hist19c/elocution.html

Ebert, R. (1997, May 31). Reviews | Great Movies
| The General. Retrieved October 25, 2023,
from Roger Ebert: https://www.rogerebert.
com/reviews/great-movie-the-general-1927

Encyclopedia Britannica. (2023, July 14). First
Battle of Bull Run. Retrieved October 14,
2023, from Britannica: britannica.com/
event/first-battle-of-bull-run-1861

Giddins, G. (2008, November 18). Buster
Keaton's "The General". Retrieved October
15, 2023, from *Slate:* https://slate.com/
culture/2008/11/why-you-really-do-need-
to-see-buster-keaton-s-the-general.html

Gindlesperger, J. (2022, March 25). The
Great Locomotive Chase: The First
Awarded Medal of Honor. Retrieved from
Congressional Medal of Honor Society:
https://www.cmohs.org/news-events/
history/the-great-locomotive-chase-the-
first-awarded-medal-of-honor/

IMDB. (n.d.). The General. Retrieved from
IMDB: https://www.imdb.com/title/
tt0017925/?ref_=nm_flmg_c_1_wr

Leonard, K. (2021, March 15). The Paratexts
of Buster Keaton's The General (1927).

Retrieved October 15, 2023, from Kendra Preston Leonard: Words for and about Music: https://kendraprestonleonard. hcommons.org/2021/03/15/paratexts-of-buster-keatons-the-general-1927/

Meade, M. (1997). *Buster Keaton: Cut to the Chase*. Da Capo Press.

Military Aviation Preservation Society (MAPS). (2022, 8 19). Official MAPS Air Museum Channel. Retrieved from William Pittenger: https://www.youtube.com/watch?v=m9V1o6MUdls

Military Heroes. (2022, 12 25). Secret Missions of the Civil War. Retrieved from https://www.youtube.com/watch?v=EE48o7lLzfQ&t=1014s

Motion Picture News. (1926, May 29). Details of United Artists' Productions: The General. *Motion Picture News*, p. 2573.

Neibaur, J. L. (2010). *The Fall of Buster Keaton: His films for MGM, Educational Pictures, and Columbia*. Scarecrow Press.

New England Journal of Education. (1880, August 26). Frontmatter. *New England Journal of Education*, 157.

Office of the Commissioner of Education. (1882). Report of the Commissioner of

Education for the Year 1880. Washington DC: Government Printing Office.

Olcott, S. (Director). (1911). *The Railroad Raiders of '62* [Motion Picture].

Philadelphia Architects and Buildings. (1880, March). National School of Elocution & Oratory. Retrieved from Philadelphia Architects and Buildings: https://www.philadelphiabuildings.org/pab/app/im_display.cfm/519151?ProjectId=-D678A34D-C749-4964-80DA741B-C10443CB

Philadelphia Inquirer. (1938, September 22). The Shoemaker School of Speech and Drama. Philadelphia Inquirer, p. 22.

Pittenger, W. (1861, July 31). Army Correspondence. Weekly Herald.

Pittenger, W. (1863). Daring and Suffering: A History of the Great Railroad Adventure. Philadelphia: J.W. Daughaday.

Pittenger, W. (1883). Extempore Speech: and how to acquire and practice it. Philadelphia: National School of Elocution and Oratory.

Pittenger, W. (1895). Toasts and Forms of Public Address for Those Who Wish to Say the Right Thing in the Right Way. Philadelphia: Penn Publishing Company.

Pittenger, W. (2023, October 11). Civil War Diaries. Retrieved from JStor: https://www.jstor.org/stable/community.30716142

Rivers, D. (1998, July 23). Pittenger Farm House. Retrieved October 25, 2023, from Fallbrook Historical Society: https://tchester.org/znet/fallbrook/history/memories/pittenger_farm_house.html

Sons of Union Veterans of the Civil War. (2008, 3 4). Sgt. William Pittenger Camp No. 21 - Our Camp's Namesake. Retrieved from Sons of Union Veterans of the Civil War: https://www.suvpac.org/camp21/pittengerbio.html

Stevens, D. (2022). Camera Man. New York: Atria Books.

Sweeney, K. W. (2007). Buster Keaton: Interviews. University of Mississippi.

The Christian Advocate. (1898, December 20). Various Topics. The Christian Advocate, p. 19.

The Historical Marker Database. (2020, 12 7). William Pittenger - Congressional Medal of Honor, 1893. Retrieved from The Historical Marker Database: https://

www.hmdb.org/m.asp?m=75887

The Victoria Warder. (1888, October 12).
Daring and Suffering. The Victoria
Warder, p. 6.

Wintermantel, M. (2014, 8 29). The Historical Marker Database. Retrieved from
William Pittenger Marker Dedication
Ceremony Program: https://www.hmdb.
org/PhotoFullSize.asp?PhotoID=284099

Young, R. N. (2018, December 31). Pastoral
Records Western Pennsylvania Conference of the United Methodist Church
1784-2018. Retrieved October 15, 2023,
from WPAUMC.org/historicalrecords:
www.wpaumc.org/historicalrecords

TOASTS

BY

WILLIAM PITTENGER

AUTHOR OF "THE DEBATER'S TREASURY"

HOW TO RESPOND TO TOASTS OR
MAKE OTHER PUBLIC ADDRESSES
AND ALWAYS SAY THE RIGHT
THING IN THE RIGHT WAY

PHILADELPHIA
THE PENN PUBLISHING COMPANY
1911

CONTENTS

INTRODUCTION

THE author of this manual has at various intervals prepared several treatises relating to the art of speech. Their wide circulation is an indication of the demand for works upon this subject. They were intended to embrace the principles which govern speech-making in the forum, in the pulpit, or at the bar. While these do not differ essentially from the principles applicable to occasions where the object is only entertainment, yet there are certain well-defined differences which it is the purpose of this little volume to point out. We hope thus to render the same service to a person who is called upon to offer or respond to a toast in a convivial assembly, as the author's previous volumes rendered to those preparing to speak upon subjects of a serious and practical nature.

That help is needed, and may be afforded, no one will deny. A novice called upon to participate in the exercises of a public banquet, an anniversary, or other entertainment, unless he has an experienced friend to give him a few hints or advice, is apt to be dismayed. He does not even know how to make a start in the work of preparation, and his sense of inability and fear of blundering go far to confuse and paralyze whatever native faculty he may have. A book like this comes to him at such a time as reinforcements to a sorely pressed army in the very crisis of a battle. As he reads, some ideas which seem practical, flash upon him. He learns what others before him have done. If he is to offer a toast, he examines the list furnished in this volume, finding one perhaps that pleases him, or one is suggested which is better adapted to his purpose than any in the book, and he wonders at the stupidity of the author in omitting it. Soon he becomes quite interested in this suggested toast, and compares it with those in the list to find out wherein it differs. Thus gradually and unconsciously he has prepared himself for the part he is to perform.

Or if invited to respond to a toast, he passes through a similar experience. He may find the outline of a speech on that very topic; he either uses it as it is printed or makes an effort to improve it by abridgment or enlargement. Next he looks through the treasury of anecdotes, selects one, or calls to mind one he has read elsewhere which he considers

better. He then studies both of them in their bearings on the subject upon which he is to speak, and longs for the hour to arrive, when he will surprise and delight his friends by his performance. He rises to speak conscious that he knows a great deal, not only about the toast assigned to him, but about other toasts as well—feels that he has something to say which, at least, will fill in the time, and save him from confusion and discredit. He even hopes to win applause by means of the stories and happy turns with which his speech is interspersed.

He has thus satisfactorily taken the first step toward becoming a ready and entertaining after-dinner speaker. The sense of knowing how to do what is expected of him has a wonderfully quieting effect upon his nerves; and thus the study of this book will greatly add to the confidence of a speaker, and the effectiveness of his delivery. Whatever graces of manner he possesses will become available, instead of being subverted by an overmastering fear.

It is not easy to mention all the uses of such a manual. One who has been accustomed to speaking, but fears he is getting into a rut, can turn to this text-book and find something which is *not* so distressingly his own, that his friends expect him to parade it before them on all occasions.

He may glance over the outline of a speech altogether new and strange to him, and endeavor to adapt
it to his own use; or he may weave together frag-
ments of several speeches, or take the framework of
one and construct upon it a speech which will enable
him to make a new departure. A writer sometimes,
after years of practice, finds it difficult to begin the
composition of some simple reception or commemora-
tive address; but the reading of a meagre outline,
not one word or idea of which may be directly used,
serves to break the spell of intellectual sloth or
inertia, and starts him upon his work briskly and
hopefully.

The field covered by the present volume is not
entirely unoccupied. One of the earliest publications in this line is an anonymous English work,
very dignified and conservative. The speeches it
furnishes are painstaking, but a trifle heavy, and
savor so much of English modes of expression, as
well as thought and customs, as to be poorly adapted
to this country. Two works have appeared in this
country, also, one being intended apparently for
wine parties only; the other, while containing a
number of gem-like little speeches, fails to give the
aid which is sought by the ordinary tyro, and is cal-
culated rather to discourage him; giving him the impression that it is more difficult to become an accept-

able after-dinner speaker than he had ever supposed.
While a few of the best things in the latter volume
are availed of, a different method is pursued in
the present work. Outlines of speeches are preferred to those which are fully elaborated; and the
few plain rules, by which a thing so informal and
easy as an after-dinner speech may be produced,
are so illustrated as to make their application almost a matter of course. Good-humor and brevity,
an outline and a story—what more is needed, unless it be that serene self-confidence which enables a
speaker to say even foolish and absurd things, with the
assurance that all goes down at a public dinner?
What if you are not the most brilliant, humorous,
and stirring speaker of the evening? Aim to fill
your place without discredit; observe closely those
who make a great success ; the next time you
may have a better outline or more telling story, and
become, before you know it, the leader of the
evening.

It is not intended to give rules or directions for
the order either of drinking or feasting. That field
is fully occupied. But the custom of making
addresses at the close of a feast has been so thoroughly established, and so frequent are these occasions, that a gentleman is not fully equipped for a
place in society, if he cannot gracefully offer or

respond to a toast, or preside at a gathering where toasts or other forms of after-dinner speaking are expected.   It is the aim of this manual to help the beginner in this field.

AFTER–DINNER SPEECHES—ANCIENT AND MODERN

An idea of the real meaning of after-dinner speaking may be obtained from the feudal feasts of earlier times. The old lord or baron of the Middle Ages partook of his principal meal in the great hall of his castle, surrounded by guests, each being assigned his place in formal order and with no small degree of ceremony. This hall was the main feature of the castle. There all the family and guests met on frequent festal occasions, and after the feasting and the hour of ceremony and more refined entertainment was over, retired to rest in comparatively small and humble apartments adjoining, though sometimes they would simply wrap their cloaks about them, and lie down to sleep on the rushes that littered the floor of the great hall.

After the "rage of hunger was appeased"—which

then, as in our day, and back even as far as the time
of the ancient Greeks, was the first business in
order—came the social hour, which meant much to
the dwellers in those dull, comfortless old barracks—
for the great castles of that day were little better
than barracks. The chief gave the signal for talk,
music, or story, previous to which, any inquiries or
conversation, other than the briefest question and
answer about the food or other necessary things,
would have been considered inappropriate and dis-
respectful. There probably was present some guest,
who came under circumstances that awakened the
strongest curiosity or who had a claim upon his en-
tertainer. Such a guest was placed at the board in a
position corresponding to his rank.

After resting and partaking of the repast, it was
pertinent to hear what account he could give of himself, and courtesy permitted the host to levy an intellectual tax upon him, as a contribution to the joy of
the hour. Seated at the head of the table the chief,
or, in his absence, a representative, made the opening
speech—the address of welcome, to use the term
familiar to ourselves. This might be very brief or at
considerable length; it might suggest inquiries of
any of the company or merely pledge an attentive
and courteous hearing to whatever the guest might
utter; it might refer to the past glory of the castle

and its lord, or vaunt its present greatness and active occupation.

But whatever form it might take it was sure to consist- -as addresses of welcome in all ages have done—of two words, by dexterously using which, any man can make a good speech of this character. These two words are "We" and "You;" and all else not connected with these is irrelevant and useless. They do not constitute two parts of the same speech but ordinarily play back and forth, like a game of battledore. Who "we" are; what "we" have done; how "we" saw "you;" what "we" have heard of "you;" how great and good "you" are thought to be; the joy at "your" coming; what "we" now want to learn of "you;" what "we" wish "you" to do; how "we" desire a longer stay or regret the need of an early departure—all is a variation of the one theme—"we" and "you."

The old Baron probably said all of this and much more in a lordly way, occupying a longer or shorter time, without ever dreaming that he was making a speech. It was his ordinary after-dinner talk to those whom chance or fortune brought within his walls. Or, if he prided himself upon being a man of few words, scorning these as fit only for women and minstrels, he would simply remind the guest that he was now at liberty to give such an account

of himself, and to prefer such requests as seemed
agreeable to him.

The guest was then expected to respond, though
this by no means was the rule.   The host might wish
first to call out more of his own intellectual treasures.
This he would do by having other occupants of the
castle speak further words of welcome, or would call
upon a minstrel to sing a song or relate some deed
of chivalry.

When the guest at last rises to speak, it is still the
two pronouns with slightly changed emphasis that
play a conspicuous part.   The "we" may become
"I;" but this is no essential change.   Where "I"
or "we" have been; what "I" have done, suffered,
or enjoyed; how and why "I" came here; how glad
"I" am to be here; what "I" have known and
heard of "you;" how "we" may help each other,
what great enterprises "we" can enter upon; how
thankful for the good cheer and good words "we"
hear.

In the baronial hall, which foreshadowed the family
fireside of later days, the drinking was free and copious whilst the other portions of the entertainment
were of a general character and quite protracted.
Mirth, song, the rude jest, anecdotes of the chase or
of a battle, or a rehearsal of the experiences of every-
day life, were all in place.   Sometimes, the guests,

overpowered by their libations, are said to have fallen under the table and to have slumbered there till surprised by the pale morning light. There was little need of ceremony in such feasts, and there is little need of formality or constraint in the far different festal occasions of the present time.

When no guest, either by chance or invitation came to the castle, less variety could be given to the after-dinner entertainment, and many expedients were required to pass the long hours that sometimes hung heavily on their hands. Then the use of "Toasts" became an important feature. The drinking also was expected to arouse interest, but if it went on in silence and gloom or amid the buzz of trivial conversation in different parts of the hall the unity of the hour was marred and the evening was voted dull—the lord himself then having no more honor than his meanest vassal. But the toast—no matter how it originated—remedied all this. A compliment and a proverb, a speech and a response, however rude, fixed the attention of every one at the table, and enabled the lord to retain the same leadership at the feast that he had won in the chase or in battle. He might himself propose a toast of his own choice or give another permission to propose it. He might then designate some humorous or entertaining clansman to respond; he might either stimulate or

2

repress the zeal of the guests, and give unity to each
part of the entertainment and to the whole feast.
For these reasons the toast rose into popularity, and
is now often used—possibly it might be said generally used if our own country alone be considered—
even when no drinking at all is indulged in.

Let us now take a look at an after-dinner hour of
the present day; one of the very latest and most approved pattern. The contrast will not be without
interest and value. The fare at the dinner is always
inviting. The company is large. Good speakers are
secured in advance. Each is given an appropriate
toast, either to propose or respond to. Suppose it is
a New England society celebrating Forefathers'
Day in New York. The chairman (who is usually
the president of the society) rises, and by touching a bell, rapping on the table, or in some other
suitable manner, attracts all eyes to himself. He
then asks the meeting to come to order, or if he prefers the form, to give attention. Then he utters a
few graceful commonplaces, and calls upon a guest to
offer the leading toast—not always the chief or most
interesting one. When one is reached in which there
is a lively interest, some distinguished person such
as Chauncey M. Depew, the prince of after-dinner
speakers, comes to the front. We give an outline of
one of his addresses on Forefathers' Day, delivered

December 22d, 1882, in response to the toast, " The Half Moon and the Mayflower."

In reading this address the " We " and " You " cannot fail to be noted. Mr. Depew said he did not know why he should be called upon to celebrate his conquerors. The Yankees had overcome the Dutch, and the two races are mingled. The speaker then introduced three fine stories—one at the expense of the Dutch who are slow in reaching their ends. A tenor singer at the church of a celebrated preacher said to Mr. Depew, " You must come again, the fact is the Doctor and myself were not at our best last Sunday morning." The second related to the inquisitiveness of a person who expressed himself thus to the guide upon the estate of the Duke of Westminster : " What, you can't tell how much the house cost or what the farm yields an acre, or what the old man's income is, or how much he is worth ? Don't you Britishers know anything ?" The third story, near the close, set off Yankee complacency. A New England girl mistook the first mile-stone from Boston for a tombstone, and reading its inscription " 1 M. from Boston," said " I'm from Boston ; how simple ; how sufficient."

The serious part of the discourse was a rapid statement of the principles represented by the Dutch **pioneer** ship " Half Moon " and the Pilgrim " May-

flower;" the elements of each contributed to national
character and progress.   (For speech in full see
Depew's Speeches, Vol. I.)

Other toasts and responses followed; eloquence and
humor mingled until the small hours of the night.
Probably not one of that pleased and brilliant assemblage for a moment thought that they were doing
at this anniversary what their old, barbaric ancestors
did nightly, while resting after a border foray or
Viking sea raid.

THE VALUE OF A GOOD STORY AND HOW TO INTRODUCE IT.

No matter how inexperienced a speaker may be or how stammering his utterance, if he can tell a good story, the average dinner party will pronounce him a success, and he will be able to resume his seat with a feeling of satisfaction. The efforts often made to bring in an entertaining story or a lively anecdote are sometimes quite amusing, but if they come in naturally the effect will unquestionably be happy. Almost any story, by using a little skill, can be adapted to nearly every occasion that may arise. We may mention a few among which a speaker can scarcely fail to find something to serve his purpose.

It is necessary always to be thoroughly familiar with the story and to understand its exact point. No matter how deliberately or with what difficulty you approach that part of your speech where the fun is to be introduced—yet, when that point *is* reached there must be no hesitation. It is well to memorize carefully the very words which express the pun, or the flash of wit or humor which is the climax of the story. The story itself may be found in such a manual as this, or in some volume of wit and humor.

There is no disadvantage in using wit gathered from any source, if it has not been so often used as to be completely worn out. When a good story is found anywhere and fully memorized and all its bearings and fine points thoroughly understood, there are two ways of getting it before an audience. The direct way is to say frankly that you have read a story and will tell it. This will answer very nicely when called upon for a speech. Few festive audiences are unwilling to accept a story for a speech, and a proposal to compromise on such terms is very likely in itself to bring applause. But the story in this case should be longer than if it is given as part of a speech. If, however, it should prove a failure, your performance will make a worse impression than when a poor story is introduced into a speech, although the story may only feebly illustrate any portion of it.

For these as well as other reasons most persons will prefer to make an address, even if it be very brief, and will endeavor to make the story fit into it. All stories that suggest diffidence, modesty, backwardness, or unwillingness to undertake great things, can be introduced to show how reluctant the speaker is to attempt a speech, and if these characteristics are only slightly referred to in the story it may still be used effectively and will leave a favorable impression.

If a topic, a toast, or a sentiment is given for a response, any of them may suggest a story; and after a good story has been told—one that has real point —it will be better to stop without making any attempt at application or explanation.

A great help is often found in the utterances of previous speakers. If these have done well, they may be complimented, and the compliment so contrived as to lead directly up to the story that is lying in wait; or something being said with which you heartily agree—however slight a portion of the address it may be—this harmony of views can be used in the same manner. On the other hand, if you disagree with any of the speakers, the mere reference to it will excite a lively interest. If this difference is used, not as the basis of a serious argument, but only to drag in a story illustrating the disagreement, the story will nevertheless appear to be very appropriate.

If you happen to be the first speaker, you are by no means without resources. You can then imagine what other speakers are going to say, and if you can slip in a humorous or good-natured hit at the expense of some of the prominent speakers, it will be highly relished. If you describe what they are likely to say it will be enjoyed, while if you should happen to mention the very opposite this will be set down as your intention. You may even describe the different speakers, and be reminded of things that will bring in the prepared story very appropriately.

The writer once knew of a very dull speaker, who scored a great success in a popular meeting, by describing the eloquent speaker who was to follow He began by telling how he was accustomed when a boy to take a skiff and follow in the wake of a steamer, to be rocked in its waves, but once getting before the huge vessel his boat was swept away, and he was nearly drowned. This unfortunately was his situation now, and he was in danger of being swept aside by the coming flood of eloquence. But he asked who is this coming man? It was the first time he had heard of him—then followed the story he had been trying to work in—a story wherein the eloquent man was described as " one who could give seventeen good reasons for anything under heaven." The story was a great success. In dumb show, the speaker he referred to begged for mercy. This only delighted the audience still more, and when the dull speaker finished it was admitted that, for once, he had escaped being stupid or commonplace. He had also forced upon the next speaker the necessity

of removing the unpleasant effects of the jokes made
at his expense, a task that required all his cleverness.

The manner of introduction by the chairman, his
name or general position, the appearance of any one
of the guests, the lateness or earliness of the hour,
events of the day that attract interest, the nature of
the entertainment or assemblage—all of these will
offer good hooks by which to draw in the story. But
let the story be good and thoroughly mastered. Of
course the work of adaptation will be much easier if
you have several stories in reserve. A story must not
be repeated so often that it becomes known as be-
longing to you, for then a preceding speaker might
get a laugh on you by telling it as yours, leaving you
bankrupt.

Jones and Smith once rode several miles in a carriage, together, to a town where both were to make
addresses. Jones was quite an orator; Smith had a
very retentive memory. Jones asked Smith about
his speech, but Smith professed not to have fully
decided upon his topic, and in turn asked Jones the
same question. Jones gave a full outline of his
speech, Smith getting him to elaborate it by judi-
cious inquiries as to how he would apply one point
and illustrate another. The ride thus passed pleasantly for both parties. Smith was called upon to
speak first, and gave with telling effect what he had

gathered from Jones, to the delight of everybody, but poor Jones, who listened in utter consternation, and had not strength enough left even to reclaim his stolen property.

If your speech is to be a story it is especially advisable to have a reserve on hand, for stories are easily copied and apt to be long remembered. Care also must be taken that the story is not one with which persons generally are familiar. A gentleman was in the habit of telling a story which has already been quoted, the point of which lies in the phrase " I'm from Boston." Some of his more intimate companions, in self-defense, would exclaim when he proposed a story, " Is it a mile from Boston?"

The definition of the toast itself or of any of the words in the sentiment which is the speaker's topic may be made the occasion for drawing in the illustrative story.

The manner of ending a good story is also worthy of careful study. When an audience is applauding a palpable " hit," it does not seem an appropriate time to stop and take one's seat; but it often is the best course. To do this appears so abrupt that the novice is apt to make a further effort to finish up the subject till he has finished up his audience as well. An attempt to fully discuss a topic, under such circumstances, is not successful once in a hundred times. The best course is to follow an apt story by some proverb, a popular reference, or a witty turn, and then to close.   But no abruptness will be disliked by your hearers half so much, as the utterance of a string of commonplaces, after you have once secured their attention.   The richness of the dessert should come at the close, not at the beginning, of the oratorical feast.

THE PURPOSE OF AFTER-DINNER
SPEAKING

Briefly stated, it is to bring into one focus the thought of an assembly. While the good things of the table may be satisfactory, and conversation free and spontaneous, there is yet need of some expedient for making all thought flow in one channel, and of blending the whole company into a true unity. There is one way, and only one, of doing this —the same that is used to produce unity of action and thought in any assembly, for whatever purpose convened. When the destinies of empires are at stake, when great questions that arise among men are to be solved, the art of speech must be called into play. So after a good dinner has been enjoyed, the same potent agency finds a field, narrower, indeed, but scarcely less operative. And this object —of causing a whole assembly to think the same thoughts and turn their attention to a common topic—is often well attained even when the speeches do not aspire to great excellence or pretension to eloquence.

28

A commonplace illustration will make our meaning clear. Suppose a great reception, where many rooms are filled with invited guests. There is conversation, but only by groups of two or three persons; refreshments are served; larger groups begin to gather around prominent persons, but there is the same diversity of sentiment and purpose that is to be found in a chance crowd in a public park. The guests are not in one place, with one accord. But now, on some pretext, the power of public speech is evoked; perhaps a toast is offered and responded to, or a more formal address of welcome or congratulation, or anything else suitable to the occasion. The subject and the manner of introduction are not material, so that the living, speaking man is brought face to face with his fellows; at once, instead of confusion and disorder, all is order and harmony The speaker may hesitate in the delivery of his message, but his very embarrassment will in some instances contribute to harmonize the thought of the assembly even more powerfully than a more pretentious address. But a good and appropriate speech will indelibly fix the thought, and be far more satisfactory.

Where no particular kind of address is indicated by the nature of the assemblage. stories and humor will generally be highly appreciated. A good story

has some of the perennial interest that surrounds a
romance, and if it is at the same time humorous, an
appeal is made to another sentiment, universal in
the human breast. If people thrill with interest in
unison, or laugh or cry together for a time, or merely
give attention to the same thoughts, there will arise
a sense of fellowship and sympathy which is not
only enjoyable, but is the very purpose for which
people are invited to assemblies.

More ordinary after-dinner speeches succeed by
the aid of humorous stories than by all other means
combined.   In a very ingenious book of ready-
made speeches the turning point of nearly every
one depends upon a pun or other trick of speech.
While this is carrying the idea a little too far, still it
fairly indicates the importance placed upon sallies
of wit or humor as a factor in speech-making.
The fellowship that comes from laughing at the
same jokes and approving the same sentiments may
not be the most intimate or the most enduring, but
it is often the only kind possible, and should be
prized accordingly.

The chief use of toasts is to call out such speeches,
and thus lead the thought of the assembly along
pleasant and appropriate channels—all prearranged,
yet apparently spontaneous.

A long speech is selfish and unpardonable. It

wearies the guests, destroys variety, and crowds others out of the places to which they have been assigned and are entitled. When the speaking is over, the company will have been led to contemplate the same themes, and will have rejoiced, sympathized, and laughed in unison.

SOME A B C DIRECTIONS FOR MAKING
SPEECHES, TOASTS, AND RESPONSES

1. Do not be afraid or ashamed to use the best helps you can get. Divest yourself of the idea that all you need is to wait till a toast is proposed and your name called, and then to open your mouth and let the eloquence flow forth. The greatest genius in the world *might* succeed in that way, but would not be likely to venture it. Use a book and study your subject well.

2. Generally, it is not well to memorize word for word either what you have written or obtained from a book, unless it is a pun or a story where the effect depends upon verbal accuracy. But be sure to memorize toasts, sentiments, and titles absolutely. To know the substance of your speech well, with one or two strong points in it, is better than to have a flowery oration weighing down your memory.

3. If you are a novice (and these directions are given to no others), do not aim to make a great speech, but to say a few things modestly and quietly. A short and unassuming speech by a beginner is sure of applause. Eloquence, if you have it in you, will come later through practice and familiarity with your subject.

4. If you can't remember or find a good story, in vent one! Perhaps you have scruples as to the latter. But a story is not a lie; if so, what would become of the noble tribe of novel-writers! Mark Twain gives a very humorous account of the way in which he killed his conscience. Probably many speakers who retail good things might make confession in the same direction.

But why is it not as reputable to invent one's own story as to tell the story some one else has invented? Does the second telling improve its morality? Rather give heed to the quality of the story. This, and not its origin, is the really important matter to consider.

5. Success in after-dinner speaking is difficult or easy to attain according to the way you go about it. If you think you must startle, rouse, and electrify your hearers, or, worse still, must instruct them in something *you* think important, but about which they care nothing, your efforts are likely to be attended by a hard and bitter experience. But if, when a prospective speech-occasion looms up, you will reflect upon the sentiment you wish to propose, or will get a friend to do a little planning and suggest the easiest toast or topic, and then attempt to

3

say just a little, you will probably come off with flying colors.

6. When you rise, do not be in a hurry. A little. hesitation has a better effect than too much promptness and fluency, and a little stammering or hesitation, it may be added, will have no bad effect. In beginning, your manner can without disadvantage be altogether lost sight of, and if you have something to say the substance of which is good, and has been carefully prearranged, you will be able to give utterance to it in some form; grammatical mistakes or mispronunciation, where there is no affectation, as well as an occasional repetition, will rarely be noticed.

7. Above all, remember it may be assumed that your hearers are your friends, and are ready to receive kindly what you have to say. This will have a wonderfully steadying effect on your nerves. And if your speech consists only of two or three sentences slowly and deliberately uttered, they will at least applaud its brevity, and give you credit for having filled your place on the programme respectably.

It has been often said that Americans are greatly ahead of the English in general speech-making, but ih pleasant after-dinner talking and addresses they are much inferior. Probably this was once true, but

If so, it is true no longer. The reason of any former deficiency was simply want of practice, without which no speech-making can be easy and effective. But the importance of this kind of oratory is now recognized, and, with proper efforts to cultivate and master it, Americans are taking the same high rank as in other forms of intellectual effort. Lowell and Depew are acknowledged as peers of any "toast-responder" or "after-dinner orator" the world has ever seen. One of the chief elements of their charm consists in the good stories they relate. Whoever has a natural faculty, be it ever so slight, as a story-teller, will, if he gathers up and appropriates the good things that he meets with, soon realize that he is making rapid progress in this delightful field, and that he gains much more than mere pleasure by his acquisitions.

The best entertainments are not those which merely make a display of wealth and luxury. Quiet, good taste, and social attractions are far better. The English wit, Foote, describes a banquet of the former character. "As to splendor, as far as it went, I admit it: there was a very fine sideboard of plate; and if a man could have swallowed a silversmith's shop, there was enough to satisfy him; but as to all the rest, the mutton was white, the veal was red, the fish was kept too long, the venison not kept long enough; to sum up all, everything was cold except the ice, and everything sour except the vinegar." Excellence in the quality of the viands is not to be disregarded in the choicest company. A celebrated scholar and wit was selecting some of the choicest delicacies on the table, when a rich friend said to him, "What! do philosophers love dainties?" "Why not?" replied the scholar; "*do you think all the good things of this world were made only for block heads?*"

HOLIDAY SPEECHES

FOURTH OF JULY

At a Fourth of July banquet, or celebration, toasts may be offered to "The Flag," to "The Day," to "Independence," to "Our Revolutionary Fathers," to "The Nation," to any Great Man of the Past, to "Liberty," to "Free Speech," to "National Greatness," to "Peace," to "Defensive War," to any of the States, to "Washington" or "Lafayette," to "Our Old Ally, France," to any of the "Patriotic Virtues," to "The Army and The Navy," to the "Memory of any of the Battles by Land or Sea." Appropriate sentiments for any of these may easily be devised or may be found in the miscellaneous list in this volume. "The Constitution and the Laws" or something similar should not be omitted.

SOME ITEMS THAT WOULD BE APPROPRIATE IN RESPONDING TO THESE TOASTS.

Their order and character will depend upon the special topic

Our present prosperity—the greatness and resources of our country as compared with those of

37

the Revolutionary epoch—the slow growth of the colonies—the rapid growth of the States and the addition of new States continually—what was gained by independence—did we do more than simply prevent tyranny—the advantages an independent country possesses over a colony, such as Canada—the perils of independence and the responsibility of power—the romantic early history of the country—the wars that preceded the Revolutionary conflict—the character of the struggle—the slenderness of our resources compared with the mighty power of Britain—our ally, France—what that nation gained and lost by joining in our quarrel—the memories of Washington and Lafayette—the principles at stake in the Revolution—the narrow view our fathers took of the issue at first, and the manner in which they were led first to independence and then to nationality—some phases of the struggle—its critical points—Trenton and Valley Forge—Saratoga and Yorktown—our responsibilities and duties—the questions of that day enumerated and compared with the burning questions of the present day (which we do not enumerate here, but which the speaker may describe or even argue if the nature of his audience, or time at his disposal permits) — the future greatness of the nation—the probability of the acquisition of new territory.

Laughable incidents either from history or illustrations from any source, must not be forgotten, for if the speech be more than a few minutes long, they are absolutely indispensable.

OUTLINE OF A SPEECH IN RESPONSE TO THE TOAST,
"THE DAY WE CELEBRATE"

The Fourth of July has been a great day ever since 1776. Before that year the Fourth of this month came and went like other days. But then a great event happened: an event which made a great difference to the entire world; the boundaries of many countries would be very different to-day if the important event of that day had not transpired. It was a terrible blow to the foes of humanity and even to many weak-kneed friends. The exhortation of one of the signers of the Declaration on that day, " We must all hang together," with the grim but very reasonable rejoinder, " If we do not, we will assuredly hang separately." The bloodshed and suffering which followed and which seem to be the only price at which human liberty and advancement can be procured. We had to deal with our old friends the English very much as the peace-loving Quaker did with the pirate who boarded his ship; taking him by the collar Broad-brim dropped him over the ship's side into the water, saying, " Friend,

thee has no business on this ship." We have shown
that we own and can navigate the ship of State ourselves, and now we are willing to welcome here not
only John Bull but all nations of the world when
they have any friendly business with us.

The gunpowder that has been consumed. First,
during the Revolutionary war and the second war
with England; and then the powder that has been
exploded by small and large boys in the hundred
and odd Fourths that have followed.

OUTLINE OF A SPREAD-EAGLE SPEECH
IN A FOREIGN LAND

We are so far from home that we can't hear the
eagle scream or see the lightning in his eye. Only
from the almanac do we know that this is the day of
all days on which he disports himself. He was a
small bird when born, more than a hundred years ago,
but has grown lively till his wings reach from ocean
to ocean, and it only requires a little faith to see him
stretch himself clear over the Western Hemisphere
and the adjacent islands. Other birds despised him
on the first great Fourth, but these birds of prey,
vultures, condors and such like, with crows, as well
as the smaller Republican eagles born since, are
humble enough to him now. The British lion himself having been so often scratched and clawed by

this fowl, has learned to shake his mane and wag his tail rather amiably in our eagle's presence, even if he has to give an occasional growl to keep his hand in. We are proud of this bird, though we are far from home, and to-day send our heartiest good wishes across the sea to the land we love the best.

OUTLINE OF A RESPONSE TO THE TOAST,
" OUR COUNTRY "

The field here is very wide. All the history of the country is appropriate, but can only be glanced at, though a good speech might be made by dwelling at length on some romantic incident in its history. The size and richness of the country from the green pine forests of Maine to the golden orange groves of California; or the prophecy of the manifest greatness of coming destiny. Here the old but laughable story can be brought in easily about the raw Irishman who saw a pumkin for the first time, and was told that it was a mare's egg, and generously given one. He had the misfortune, however, to drop it out of his cart, when it rolled down-hill, struck a stump, burst and frightened a rabbit, which bounded away followed by Pat, shouting: "Shtop my colt; sure and if he is so big and can run so fast now, when just born, what a rousing horse he will be when grown up!"

But our country has more than merely a vast area.

She has made advances in science, art, literature, and culture of all kinds, and is destined to play a chief part in the drama of the world's progress.

MEMORIAL DAY

The celebration of this day has become general and has assumed a special and beautiful character. It might have been feared that angry passions engendered by civil strife would predominate, but the very reverse of this is true. Kindness and charity, tender memories of the sacrifices of patriotism, the duty of caring for the living and of avoiding all that might lead again to the sad necessity of war, are the sentiments nearly always inculcated.

The following are a few of the toasts that may be given at celebrations, or banquets, or at the exercises that form a part of the annual decorating of soldiers' graves:

The Martyred Dead—the Regiments locally represented—the Army and Navy—any Dead Soldier especially prominent—the Union Forever—the Whole Country—Victory always for the Right—the Surviving Soldiers and Sailors—Unbroken Peace—the Commander-in-Chief, and other officers locally honored—any special battle whose field is near at hand—the Flag with all its Stars undimmed.

SKETCH OF A SPEECH IN RESPONSE TO THE TOAST,

"OUR HONORED DEAD"

Time in its rapid flight tests many things. Thirty years ago the Southern Confederacy, like a dark cloud full of storm and thunderings, covered the Southern heavens. Statesmen planned, preachers prayed, women wept, and armies as brave as ever formed in line fought, for its establishment. Blood flowed freely, and the roar of battle filled the whole land. Many wise men thought it would continue for ages, but lo! it has disappeared. Nothing remains to its adherents but a memory—mournful, pathetic, and bitter.

How different with the Old Flag that we love. It had been tested before, but this was its supreme trial. It had been victorious in several wars. It had sheltered new and expanding States, it had fostered higher forms of civilization, and represented peoples and interests that were complex and varied; but in our Civil War it was assailed as never before. The test was crucial, but nobly was it borne. Men died in ranks as the forest goes down before the cyclone. What sharp agony in death, and what long-continued suffering and bereavement this implies. But the result was decisive—a strengthening of the power and grandeur of the nation that sometimes seems to be only too great and unquestioned.

We have no wish by any word of ours to revive bitter feeling or stir up strife. This hallowed day has been from the first a peacemaker. Men, standing with uncovered heads in the presence of the dead, do not care to utter words of reproach for the irrevocable past. We, wearing the blue, can say to the scarred veteran wearers of the gray: "You fought well for the lost cause. But the case was fairly tried in the awful court of war. It took four years for the jury to agree, but the verdict has been given— a verdict against your cause—and there is no higher court and no appeal. There is no resurrection for the dead Confederacy; but we can offer you something better—an equal part in the life and destiny of the most glorious nation time has yet produced." And on their side the gray can reply, in the words of Colonel Grady, the eloquent orator of the South, in his speech at Atlanta: "We can now see that in this conflict loss was gain, and defeat real and substantial victory; that everything we hoped for and fought for, in the new government we sought to establish, is given to us in greater measure in the old government our fathers founded."

We do not meet on these Memorial Days to weep for the dead, as we did while wounds were yet fresh.

Time has healed the scars of war, and we can calmly contemplate the great lesson of patriotic devotion, and rejoice that the nation to which we belong produced men noble enough to die for that which they valued so much. Neither do I care to say anything of human slavery, the institution that died and was buried with the Confederacy. I had enough to say about it while it was living. Let the dead past bury its dead.

But we are here to foster patriotism, in view of the most tremendous sacrifice ever willingly made by a people on the altar of nationality. That the sacrifices of the Civil War deserve this rank will appear from the fact that they were made—in the main—by volunteers. We were not fighting directly to defend our altars and our fires; we were not driven to arms to repel an invading foe; we were not hurried to the field by king or noble; but in the first flush of manhood we offered ourselves to preserve unimpaired the unity, the purity, the glory of our nation. So far as I have turned over the leaves of the volume of time, I have found nothing in all the past like this. Therefore, standing before the highest manifestation of earthly patriotism, viewing it crowned in all the glory of self-sacrifice, by a faithfulness which was literally in the case of hundreds of thousands " unto death," we ask : " What is there

that justifies a nation in exacting or accepting (when
freely offered) such tribute of the life-blood of its
people ?"

The two things of inestimable value which our
government furnishes and which we ought to preserve
even with life itself, if the sacrifice is needed, are
liberty and law, or rather liberty *in* law. The old
world gave law, without which human society cannot
exist. But it was accompanied with terrible suffering—as when " order reigned in Warsaw." Such law
came from masters, and made the mass of the people
slaves. We have an equal perfection of law, order,
subordination, but it rises side by side with liberty
The people govern themselves—not in one form of
government alone but in affairs national, State,
county, down to the smallest school district and a
thousand voluntary societies. In each the methods
by which the people's will may be made supreme in
designated affairs are clearly defined, so that the whole
of united human effort is brought under the do
minion of law, even such things as general education, and yet each affair is in the hands of the people
directly concerned. For thousands of years the
principles of our complex and wonderful system of
co-ordinated government have been growing up till
they have reached their fullest perfection on our soil,
and we breathe their beneficence as we breathe the air

of heaven. Men are willing to die by the tens of thousands that this liberty under law may not perish from the world.

. . . Comrades and Citizens:—We move forward to new issues and new responsibilities. Grave dangers are now upon us. God grant that they may not need to be met and settled in the rude shock of war. The time for wisdom, for clear-sighted patriotism is—*now*. Labor and capital, the foundations of law and order; the complex civilization of a nation which now talks by lightning, and is hurled by steam over plains and mountains, and which, doubtless, will soon fly through the air—all these are to be settled by the men now on the stage of action. We cannot do better than to tell you, to settle them in the spirit of the men whose great sacrifices we to-day commemorate.

OUTLINE OF A SPEECH BY CHAUNCEY M. DEPEW, ON
A DECORATION [MEMORIAL] DAY

This is one of the most interesting of national celebrations, appealing not to pride, but to tender personal memories. But we must not give ourselves up wholly to sadness or mourning. The story of issues and results must be told.

Why did our heroes die? On account of the cancer of slavery and the resulting doctrine of State

Rights. Nationality and liberty, the opposite view.
The former was the party of action, and, therefore,
though in a minority, it was bolder and more determined. But the shell of materialism dropped from
the North, and it was aroused with electric energy
when Sumter was fired on; there was no passion,
only such fervid resolve to preserve our nation as the
world never before saw. The struggle over, there were
no State trials, no prisons nor scaffolds, and the Republic, though bleeding at every pore, said to the
conquered enemy, "Come and share fully with us all
the blessings of our preserved institutions," and thus
won a second victory greater than the first.

The wonderful intelligence of the volunteer—
story of Napoleon's soldier—"Dead on the field of
honor."

The Grand Army of the elect—the heroes of
history, some of whom are enumerated—the actual
value to a nation of such heroism. To-day all that
belongs to the strife is forgiven, but its lessons are too
noble and precious ever to be forgotten. We can all,
North and South, read with enthusiasm the story of
each varied and romantic campaign.

The Confederate women first began decorating the
graves of their dead with flowers, and did not pass
by the Union graves near their late foes. This
touched the heart of the nation as nothing else could

have done, and enmity melted away, and the observance of the day has become universal.

The two great national heroes—Washington, with his wise, foresighted " Farewell Address ;" Lincoln, with his gentle spirit, his martyr death, and his tender words, " With malice towards none, with charity for all." Washington the Founder, Lincoln the Preserver.

WASHINGTON'S BIRTHDAY

APPROPRIATE TOASTS

To Washington—to The Great Men of Revolutionary Times—to The Great Man who could not do what many modern Politicians can do—*tell a lie*—to The Childless Father of Eighty Millions of people— to The American Model Statesman—to The Greatest of Good Men and the Best of Great Men.

THOUGHTS FOR A SPEECH IN RESPONSE TO THE TOAST " WASHINGTON : GREAT AS A SOLDIER, GREATER AS A STATESMAN, GREATEST AS A PURE PATRIOT "

Indian, French, and English enemies. He had to make the armies with which he conquered. He was always a safe commander, but full of enterprise also— his character made the Union of the States and the

4

Constitution possible. His character the best inherit-
ance of the American people. Other men as great,
possibly in some instances greater in a single field—
his greatness shown in the wide union of the noblest
kinds of greatness, all in harmony.

HUMOROUS RESPONSE BY BENJAMIN F. BUTLER TO THE
TOAST, "OUR FOREFATHERS"

"While venerating their lofty patriotism, may we
emulate them in their republican simplicity of manners." He declared that a great deal had been said
at one time and another about the democratic simplicity of our forefathers. Suppose that the gentlemen of the present day should go back to some of the
customs of the forefathers. Suppose a man should go
to a ball nowadays in the costume in which Thomas
Jefferson, "that great apostle of democratic simplicity," once appeared in Philadelphia. What a
sensation he would create with his modest (?) costume of velvet and lace, with knee-breeches, silk
stockings, silver shoe-buckles, and powdered wig.
"Even the great father of his country had a little
style about him," said the speaker. "It was a known
fact that he never went to Congress when he was President unless he went in a coach and six, with a little
cupid on the box bearing a wreath of flowers. The
coach must be yellow and the horses white, and then

the President's secretary usually followed in a coach drawn by four horses. When Washington ascended the steps to enter the doors, he always stopped for a moment and turned slowly around to allow an admiring people to see the father of their country. Oh! our forefathers were saturated with modesty and simplicity. The people of the present day have retrograded greatly from the simplicity of their Revolutionary ancestors. I can remember when it was impossible, years before the war, to hold a night session of Congress. It was impossible because the members of Congress attended dinners, and lingered over their wine. They attended dinners very like the one we have just enjoyed, and yet there is not a man in this company who is unfitted to attend to any public or private duties that might demand his attention. Yes, it is true that we have departed from the old customs, but we have advanced and not retrograded. The world has changed, but it has changed for the better. It is growing better every day, and don't let anybody forget it."

CHRISTMAS

APPROPRIATE TOASTS

The Day of Good-will—to The Cold Weather without and the Warm Hearts within—to The Christmas

Tree, which grows in a Night and is plucked in the
Morning by the gladdest of fingers—to The Day in
which Religion gives sweetness to Social Life—
Christmas Gifts; may they bless the Giver not less
than the Receiver—to The Oldest of our Festivals,
which grows mellower and sweeter with the passage
of the centuries—to St. Nicholas [or Santa Claus],
the only saint Protestants worship—to A Merry Day
that leaves no heart-ache—to A Good Christmas,
may sleighing, gifts, and feasting crowd out all
gambling and drunkenness.

SPEECH-THOUGHTS

The good cheer enjoyed on this merriest day of the
year. How the little people look forward to it. It
comes to the older ones as a joy, and yet tender and
sad with the memories of other Christmases. The
religious and the secular elements of the day. The
countries where it is most observed. The long contest
between the two days, Thanksgiving and Christmas
The compromise that Massachusetts and Virginia.
New England and the South, have unanimously
agreed upon; namely, to keep both days.

SELECTED OUTLINE OF AN EFFECTIVE LITTLE CHRISTMAS SPEECH

The speaker assumes that the observance of the
day is becoming obsolete, and that there are persons

who wish it to die out. The assumption, though rather strained, affords the opportunity to demolish this man of straw. "All other kings may go, but no one can spare King Christmas, or St. Nicholas, his prime minister. School-rooms and nurseries would rebel. And plum pudding is too strongly entrenched in Church and State to be dislodged. Washington Irving, with his *Sketch Book*, would protest. Best argument of all is the worth of the Christmas entertainments. Here's to the Festival of Festivals, and long may its honors be done by such hosts as entertain us to-day."

THANKSGIVING

Coming at the beginning of the farmer's rest, when the harvest is all gathered, this is a very joyous festival, and more than any other abounds in family reunions. Any toast therefore is appropriate which tells of the harvest, of fertility, of the closing year, of the family pride and traditions, of pleasure to young and old. At dinner, turkey and mince or pumpkin pie will of course be served, and these national favorites must not be forgotten by the toast-maker.

This day, too, has an official and governmental flavor given to it by the State and national proclamations which fix the date and invite its observance. Usually, these enumerate the blessings enjoyed by the whole country during the year, and suggest topics peculiarly fitting for toasts. It is perhaps not too much to say that Thanksgiving is distinctly *the* American Festival, and should be honored accordingly.

TOASTS

To The Inventor of Pumpkin Pie—to Peace with all Nations—to The Rulers of our Country—to The Farmer—to Full Stomachs and Merry Hearts—to their Excellencies, the President and the Governor; may we obey all their commands as willingly as when they tell us to feast—Abounding Plenty; may we always remember the Source from which our benefits come—Our two National Fowls, the American Eagle and the Thanksgiving Turkey; may the one give us peace for all our States and the other a piece for all our plates—The Turkey and the Eagle; we love to have the one soar high, but wish the other to roost low—The Great American Birds; may we have them where we love them best, the Turkeys on our tables and the Eagles in our pockets.

THOUGHTS FOR A THANKSGIVING SPEECH

The manner in which the day was first instituted. The sore struggles and the small beginnings of that day compared with the greatness and abounding prosperity of the present. The warfare between Christmas and Thanksgiving, the one being thought the badge of popery and prelacy. The Battle of the Pies, pumpkin and mince, terminating in a treaty of peace and alliance; and now we can enjoy the nightmare by feasting on both combined! The national blessings of the year; the poorest have more now than kings and emperors had five hundred years ago. Exemption from wars. Internal peace. Willingness and habit of settling every domestic dispute by the ballot, and not the bullet. The increasing tendency to arbitrate between nations, thus avoiding the horrors of war. The beneficence of our government and the ease with which its operations rest upon our shoulders. The wonderful progress of science and invention, and the manner in which these have added to the comfort of all the people.

SELECTED OUTLINE FOR A THANKSGIVING SPEECH

Why we ought to be grateful to the old Puritans, with all their faults. Their unsuccessful warfare on plum pudding, which, like truth, " crushed to earth," rose again. Their discovery and enshrining of Turkey. On this day the Nation gathers as a family at the Thanksgiving board, and from all parts of the world the wanderers come home to the family feast. The duty of Happiness, joined to gratitude, is emphasized this day. The closing toast, " The Federal Eagle and the Festal Turkey; may we always have peace under the wings of the one, and be able to obtain a piece from the breast of the other."

PRESENTATION ADDRESSES

Giving a present is a kind and graceful act, and should be accompanied by a simple, short, and unaffected speech. "Take this" would have the merit of brevity, but would fail in conveying any information as to *who* gave, why they gave *to the recipient*, and why *that* present was selected rather than another, and why *the speaker* was chosen to make the presentation. All of these items form a part of nearly every presentation address, whilst some of them belong to all.

The novice will find much help in preparing his proposed speech by selecting a few items that are generally appropriate ; afterward he can include anything which his own genius or wishes may suggest.

He may say that an abler speaker might have been selected for the pleasant duty, but not one who could enter into it more heartily or with more good wishes. He can refer to any circumstance which, if told briefly, will show why he has been selected, notwithstanding his reluctance or sense of unworthiness; or why he is pleased that the selection has fallen upon him. Such reference is usually effective.

Then the nature of the gift may be described. Here is an easy field for a little pleasantry. If a watch, it can be said, "Your friends are growing a little suspicious of you, and, after due deliberation, they have determined to a place *a watch* upon you.' If a cane is the article in hand, then the painful duty of administering punishment for offenses by *caning* is in order. A ring will afford an opportunity for many verbal plays. The ring of friends about the recipient, the true ring of a bell, or of an uncracked vase, a political ring—any of these can be made to lead up to the little hoop of gold. The fineness of the material, its sterling and unvarying value, the inscription on it, any specialty in its form —all these will be found rich in suggestion. Silverware of any kind may also be considered as to the form of the article, the use to which it is to be put, and the purity of the metal. Hardly any article can be thought of which will not allow some pleasant puns or *bon mots*. If a book is given, we bring the person "to book," and the book to him. Job wished that his enemy might write a book; we, more charitable, wish our friend to read a book, and now offer him a good one for the purpose. The author or the title will, if closely examined, yield some matter for play on words.

The army presents of sword or banner, while usually more serious, do not forbid the same kind of badinage.

But this should form only a small portion of the speech, and consist merely of two or three well-studied sentences, to be uttered slowly, so that their double meaning may have time to sink in, and appear also as if they were just thought of. A good anecdote should be introduced at this point. It must be short, tinged with humor, and, if it succeeds in arousing the attention of the hearers, it will be of great value. If it is very appropriate or highly illustrative, these qualities will compensate for humor. Indeed, a felicitous anecdote will make the whole speech a success, if the speech is not continued too long afterward. Better suffer the extreme penalty of reading every anecdote in this volume, and of searching for hours in other fields, than fail to get the right one; but if unsuccessful invent one for the occasion!

The good qualities of the recipient must not be overlooked, especially those in recognition of which the present is given. If anything in the nature of the present itself can be made symbolic of these assumed good or great qualities, it will be a happy

circumstance. And while flattery should not be
excessive or too palpable, it is seldom indeed that
a large dose of "pleasant things" will not be well
received by all parties on such an occasion.

The expression of kindly feeling and good wishes
always affords a favorable opportunity for closing
Perhaps, however, a more striking conclusion can
be made by taking advantage of the very moment
when the present is handed over to the recipient,
accompanying this act with a hearty wish for its
long retention and its happy use in the manner its
nature indicates. Wishing a ring to be worn as a
memento of friendship, a watch to mark the passage
of happy hours, a cane not to be needed for support,
but only as a treasured ornament, a sword to be worn
with honor and only to be unsheathed at the call of
duty or of patriotism, etc.

The reception of a gift is more easy than the presentation, but is at the same time more embarrassing.
The reception is easier, because the essential part of
the response is to say "Thank you," which are very
easy words to utter if the givers are real friends and
the present is an appropriate one. It is more embarrassing because it is always harder to receive a
favor gratefully than to give one. If the gift is a
surprise, there is no harm in saying so, though if
it is not a surprise, it is not advisable to tell an

untruth about it. The recipient may say he is em-
barrassed, and his embarrassment—whether real or
feigned—will create sympathy for him. Besides, he
can ask for indulgence with more grace than the
preceding speaker, as he is supposed to be taken by
surprise. He may be so overcome with emotion
as to break down altogether, and yet he will be
loudly applauded.

A still stronger reason for this disparity is that the
speaker representing the givers has been selected,
probably out of a large company, to make his speech,
and is thus expected to do it well; but the receiver
occupies *his* position for a reason that has no connection whatever with his speech-making powers.
If he succeeds in expressing his gratitude and good-
will to those who have been so generous he will have
served the essential purpose of his speech; but if,
in addition, he can gather up the points made in
the presentation speech, assenting to its general principles, accepting the humorous charges for which he
is to be watched, caned, stoned (when a diamond
or other stone is given), or put to the sword, and
gently deprecates the serious flattery offered, he will
be regarded as doing exceedingly well. One phrase
he will not be likely to omit, unless " he loses his
head" altogether—" When I look upon this, I will

always remember the feelings of this hour, the kind words uttered, the appreciation shown." This word " appreciation," with the reiteration of thanks, will make a very fitting conclusion.

ADDRESSES OF WELCOME

In our country the number of voluntary associations that visit similar associations, or meet at special
times and places is very large. Often such associations are furnished with free board and lodging by
the people of the place where the assemblage occurs.
Facilities for assemblage and enjoyment are offered
and other privileges tendered that are highly appreciated. Religious bodies, church and philanthropic
societies, military and fire companies, athletic and
social clubs, various orders and educational societies,
political bodies, these form only a small proportion
of the endless number of organizations convening
and gathering at different centres, gatherings which
serve to keep all parts of our country in close touch.

It is needless to furnish model speeches for each
of these, for the same general line of remark is
adapted to all. The changes of illustration demanded by the character of the association to be
welcomed, and for which responses are to be made,
will be readily understood, and a little study of the
name and character of the place of meeting will

make the necessary local allusions quite easy. The welcome and response for a fire company, or a base-ball club, will not differ much from that for a Christian Endeavor Society. A few general hints and a little investigation by the novice will put him on the right track in either case.

ADDRESS OF WELCOME

A clear statement about those who extend the welcome and of those who are to be welcomed is appropriate. This may be expanded advantageously by giving a few of the characteristics of each, greater latitude being allowed in complimenting those who are welcomed than those who entertain. It is bad taste to spend more time in telling our guests how good and great we are than in expressing the exalted opinion we have of them for their noble work, their great fame, or their high purpose; or in declaring the pleasure we feel and the honor we have in entertaining them. The warmth of the welcome extended should be expressed in the fullest manner, and as this is the central purpose of the whole address, it will bear *one repetition*. A good illustrative story, brief but pointed, may be worked in somewhere, perhaps in connection with a modest depreciation of our own fitness or ability adequately to express the strong feelings of those we represent, though if one can be found having a connection with the visitors themselves, it will be still better. What we wish our visitors to do while with us may also be appropriately referred to. If there are places of interest for them to visit, work for them to do, or special entertainments provided,—here is additional matter for remark. All these items may be run through in a few minutes, and then the address should close. The most bungling and formal welcome, if short, will be enjoyed more and be more applauded than the most graceful and eloquent one unduly prolonged. Should, however, in spite of this warning, more " filling in " be desired of an appropriate character, it may be found almost without limit in setting forth the claims of the cause which both the visitors and the entertainers represent—athletic sports, religion, benevolence, education, or what not.

ADDRESS IN RESPONSE

This may be still more brief than the address of welcome. To say that the reception is hearty, that it gives pleasure and is gratefully received and appreciated, is all that is essential. An invitation to return the visit should not be forgotten, if circumstances are such that it can be appropriately made. Then the speaker has an opportunity to review any portion of the preceding speech and express his indorse-

5

ment of any of the assertions made.   He should not
dissent from them, unless this dissent can be made the
means of a little adroit flattery by placing a higher
estimate upon the entertainers and their services
than their own speaker has done, or by modestly
disclaiming some of the praise that has been given.
The novice must avoid being carried too far by this
fascinating review, both as to the quantity and the
quality of the disagreement.

A closing sentence may be, "Allow me once more,
most heartily, to thank you for this generous welcome to—your homes—your headquarters—to the
hospitalities of your city," as the case may be.

WEDDING AND OTHER ANNIVERSARIES

Another wide field for the oratory of entertainment is to be found in the various celebrations that mark the passage of specific or notable portions of time—centennial, semi-centennial, and quadrennial; likewise weddings, annual, tin, paper, crystal, silver, and golden. The speeches for these differ widely in character. They may take the form of congratulatory addresses, of toasts and responses, or more formal addresses. All dedications come in the same category. Generally the shorter intervals call for light and humorous speeches, while the longer ones demand something more grave and thoughtful.

The following speech and response for a wooden (fifth) wedding anniversary is taken from a volume of ready made speeches. It is a fine example of that wit and play upon words which is never more suitable or more highly appreciated than on such an occasion.

SPEECH FOR A WOODEN WEDDING

If it is a good maxim not to halloo till you are out of the woods. our kind host and hostess must be very quiet this evening, for it seems to me that they are in the thick of it. If their friends had been about to burn them alive instead of to wish them joy on their fifth wedding-day, they could scarcely have brought a greater quantity of combustible material to the sacrifice. What shall we say to them on this ligneous occasion? Of course, we must congratulate them on their willingness to renew their matrimonial vows after five years of double-blessedness. In this age of divorce it is something worthy of note, that a pair who have been one and inseparable for even so short a period as the twentieth part of a century, should stand up proudly before the world and propose to strengthen the original compact with a new one. They look as happy and contented as if they had never heard of Chicago, or seen those tempting little advertisements in the newspapers that propose to separate man and wife with immediate dispatch for a reasonable consideration. Instead of going to court to cut the nuptial bond in twain, it appears that they have been *courting* for five years with the view of being remarried this evening. Vaccination, it is said, wears out in seven years, but matrimony, we see, in this instance, at least, takes a stronger hold of the parties inoculated as time rolls on; and although in this case they are willing to go through the operation again, it is not for the sake of making assurance doubly sure, but in order to enjoy marriage as a luxury. With this happy specimen of a wooden wedding before them, our young unmarried friends will see that they can go into the *joinery* business with but little risk of getting into the wrong box. In fact, it is because connubial bliss beats every other species of felicity all hollow that we have met this evening to requite it with hollow-ware. In the name of all their friends, I affectionately congratulate the doubly-married pair on their past happiness and future prospects, and hope they may live to celebrate their fiftieth wedding-day and receive a *golden* reward.

BRIDEGROOM IN REPLY

"For self and partner"—as men associated in business sometimes conclude their letters—I offer to you and all our friends who have obliged us with their presence, the thanks of the firm which renews its articles of partnership this evening. We welcome you heartily to our home, well knowing that your kind wishes are not like—your useful and elegant tokens of remembrance—*hollow-ware*. When Birnam Wood came to Dunsinane, Macbeth was conquered, and it seems to me that you have come almost as well provided with timber as Macduff and Malcolm were. Your articles, however, although of wood, are not of the Burn 'em kind, and I am not such a Dunce inane as to decline accepting them. Indeed, my wife, who, notwithstanding her matrimonial vows, has a *single eye*—to housekeeping—would not permit me to refuse them were I so inclined. She knows their value better than I do, and with the assistance of her kitchen cabinet will, I have no doubt, employ them usefully.

The speech closes with thanks and good wishes in return.

TOASTS

A toast may be given either with or without a sentiment attached, and in either case a response is equally fitting; but in the former the subject is narrowed and defined by the nature of the sentiment. Yet the speaker need not hold himself closely to the sentiment, which is often made rather a point of departure even by the ablest speakers. Indeed, the latitude accorded to after-dinner speeches is very great, and a sentiment which gives unity and direction to the speech made in response to it is, on that account, of great value.

To illustrate these points we will take the toast, "Our Flag." A speech in response would be practically unlimited in scope of treatment. Anything patriotic, historical or sentimental, which brings in some reference to the banner, would be appropriate. But let this sentiment be added: "May the justness and benevolence which it represents ever charm the heart, as its beauty charms the eye," and the outline of a speech is already indicated. Has our nation always been just and kind? Where and how have

these qualities been most strikingly manifested?
Why have we seemed sometimes to come short of
them, and how should such injustice or harsh dealing be remedied, with as much rhetorical admixture
of the waving folds and the glittering stars as the
speaker sees fit to employ.

From these considerations may be deduced the
rule that when the proposer of a toast wishes to
leave the respondent the freedom of the whole subject he will give the toast alone, or accompanied by
a motto of the most non-committal character. But
if he wishes to draw him out in a particular direction he will put the real theme in the sentiment
that follows the toast.

SENTIMENTS SUGGESTED BY A TOAST

Years ago a speaker provoked a controversy (ma-
liciously and with no good excuse) which scarcely
came short of blows, by proposing as a toast the name
of a general of high rank, but who was unfortunate
in arms. He was a candidate for office. Added to
the toast was the sentiment, " May his political equal
his military victories." This was in bad taste, indeed, but it shows the use that can be made of the
sentiment, when added to a toast, in fixing attention
in a certain direction.

The number of sentiments suggested by the common and standard toasts is unlimited. Take the toast " Home," as an example.

Home: The golden setting in which the brightest jewel is " Mother."

Home: A world of strife shut out, and a world of love shut in.

Home: The blossoms of which heaven is the fruit.

Home: The only spot on earth where the faults and failings of fallen humanity are hidden under a mantle of charity.

Home: An abode wherein the inmate, the superior being called man, can pay back at night, with fifty per cent. interest, every annoyance that he has met with in business during the day.

Home: The place where the great are sometimes small, and the small often great.

Home: The father's kingdom; the child's paradise; the mother's world.

Home: The jewel casket containing the most precious of all jewels—domestic happiness.

Home: The place where you are treated best and grumble most.

Home: It is the central telegraph office of human love, into which run innumerable wires of affection, many of which, though extending thousands of miles, are never disconnected from the one great terminus.

Home: The centre of our affections, around which our hearts' best wishes twine.

Home: A little sheltered hollow scooped out of the windy hill of the world.

Home: A place where our stomachs get three good meals daily and our hearts a thousand.

MISCELLANEOUS TOASTS

These might be multiplied indefinitely, but a sufficient number are given to serve as hints to the person who is able to make his own toasts, yet seeks a little aid to lift him out of the common rut.

Marriage: The happy estate which resembles a pair of shears; so joined that they cannot be separated; often moving in opposite directions, yet always punishing any one who comes between them.

Marriage: The gate through which the happy lover leaves his enchanted ground and returns from paradise to earth.

Woman: The fairest work of the great Author; the edition is large, and no man should be without a copy.

Woman: She needs no eulogy; she speaks for herself.

Woman: The bitter half of man. (A sour bachelor's toast.)

Wedlock: May the single all be married and all the married be happy. Love to one, friendship to many, and good-will to all.

The Lady we love and the Friend we trust.

May we have the unspeakable good Fortune to win a true heart, and the Merit to keep it.

Friendship: May its bark never founder on the rocks of deception.

Friendship: May its lamp ever be supplied by the oil of truth and fidelity.

Unselfish Friendship: May we ever be able to serve a friend, and noble enough to conceal it.

Firm Friendship: May differences of opinion only cement it.

May we have more and more Friends and Need them less and less.

May our Friend in sorrow never be a Sorrowing friend.

Active Friendship: May the hinges of friendship never grow rusty.

To our Friends: Whether absent on land or sea.

Our Friends: May the present have no burdens for them and futurity no terrors.

Our Friends: May we always have them and always know their value.

Friends: May we be richer in their love than in wealth, and yet money be plenty.

A Friend: May we never want one to cheer us, or a home to welcome him.

Good Judgment: May opinions never float in the sea of ignorance.

Careful Kindness: May we never crack a joke or break a reputation.

Enduring Prudence: May the pleasures of youth never bring us pain in old age.

Deliverance in Trouble: May the sunshine of hope dispel the clouds of calamity.

Successful Suit: May we court and win all the Daughters of Fortune except the eldest—Miss Fortune.

Here's a Health to Detail, Retail, and Curtail— indeed, all the tails but tell-tales.

The Coming Millennium: When great men are honest and honest men are great.

Our Merchant: May he have good trade, well paid.

   May the Devil cut the toes of all our foes,

   That we may know them by their limping.

May we Live to learn well and Learn to live well.

A Placid Life: May we never murmur without cause, and never have cause to murmur.

May we never lose our Bait when we Fish for compliments.

A Better Distribution of Money: May Avarice lose his purse and Benevolence find it.

May Care be a stranger and Serenity a familiar friend to every honest heart.

May Fortune recover her eyesight and be able to distribute her gifts more wisely and equally.

May Bad Example never attract youthful minds.

May Poverty never come to us without rich compensations and hope of a speedy departure.

Our Flag: The beautiful banner that represents the precious *mettle* of America.

American Eagle, The: The liberty bird that permits no liberties.

American Eagle, The: May she build her nest in every rock peak of this continent.

American Valor: May no war require it, but may it be always ready for every foe.

American People, The: May they live in peace and grow strong in the practice of every virtue.

Our Native Land: May it ever be worthy of our heartiest love, and continue to draw it forth without stint.

(A spread-eagle toast.) The Boundaries of Our Country: East, by the Rising Sun; north, by the North Pole; west, by all Creation; and south, by the Day of Judgment.

Our Lakes and Rivers: Navigable waters that unite all the States and render the very thought of their separation absurd.

Our Sons and Daughters: May they be honest as brave and modest as fair.

America and the World: May our nation ever enjoy the blessings of the widest liberty, and be ever ready to promote the liberties of mankind.

Discontented Citizens: May they speedily leave their country for their country's good.

America:

" Our hearts, our hopes are all with thee,
    Our hearts, our hopes, our prayers, our tears,
    Our faith, triumphant o'er our fears,
  Are all with thee, are all with thee."

The Patriot:

" Breathes there a man with soul so dead,
    Who never to himself hath said,
      This is my own, my native land;
    Whose heart hath ne'er within him burned,
    As home his footsteps he hath turned
      From wandering on a foreign strand?"

Our Country: Whether bounded by Canada or Mexico, or however otherwise bounded and described; be the measurement more or less, still Our Country; to be cherished in our hearts and defended by our lives.

Our Country: In our intercourse with foreign

nations may she always be in the right; and if not, may we ever be true patriots enough to get her into the right at any cost.

Our Country: May we render due reverence and love to the common mother of us all.

The Ship of State:

> " Nail to the mast her holy flag;
> Set every threadbare sail;
> And give her to the God of Storms,
> The lightning and the gale."

Columbia: My country, with all thy faults, I love thee still.

Webster's Motto: Liberty and Union, now and forever, one and inseparable.

True Patriotism: May every American be a good citizen in peace, a valiant soldier in war.

Our Country: May our love of country be without bounds and without a shadow of fear.

Our Statesmen: May they care less for party and for personal ambition than for the nation's welfare.

Failure to Treason: May he who would destroy his country for a mess of pottage never get the pottage!

The Penalty of Treason: May he who would uproot the tree of Liberty be the first one crushed by its fall.

The Nation: May it know no North, no South, no

East, no West, but only one broad, beautiful, glorious land.

America:

Dear Country, our thoughts are more constant to
        thee,
Than the steel to the star and the stream to the sea.

Our Revolutionary Fathers: May their sons never disgrace their parentage.

Our Town: The best in the land; let him that don't like it leave it.

The Tree of Liberty: May every American citizen help cultivate it and eat freely of its fruit.

The Emigrant: May the man that doesn't love his native country speedily hie him to one that he can love.

The American Eagle: It is not healthful to try to deposit salt on his venerable tail.

California: The land of golden rocks and golden fruits.

Ohio: The second Mother of Presidents.

Vermont: A State of rocks, but producing men, women, maple sugar, and horses.

" The first are strong, the last are fleet,
    The second and third are exceedingly sweet,
    And all are uncommonly hard to beat."

Texas: The biggest of States, and one of the very best.

New York: Unrivalled if numbers in city and State be the test.

Our Navy: May it always be as anxious to preserve peace as to uphold the honor of the flag in war.

Our Army: May it ever be very small in peace, but grow to mighty dimensions and mightier achievements in war.

Our Country: May the form of liberty never be used to subvert the principles of true freedom.

Our Voters: May they always have a standard to try their rulers by, and be quick to punish or reward justly.

Fortune: A divinity to fools, a helper to wise men.

The Present: Anticipation may be very agreeable, but participation is more practical.

The Present Opportunity: We may lay in a stock of pleasures for use in memory, but they must be kept carefully to prevent mouldering.

Philosophy: It may conquer past or present pain; but toothache, while it lasts, laughs at philosophy.

Our Noble Selves: Why not toast ourselves and praise ourselves since we have the best means of knowing all the good in ourselves?

Charity: A link from the chain of gold that angels forge.

6

Our Harvests: May the sunshine of plenty dispel the clouds of care.

Virtue: May we have the wit to discover what is true and the fortitude to practice what is good.

Our Firesides: Our heads may not be sharpened at colleges, but our hearts are graduates of the hearths.

The True Medium: Give us good form, but not formality.

The Excesses of Youth: They are heavy drafts upon old age, payable with compound interest about thirty years from date.

The Best of Good Feeling: May we never feel want nor want feeling.

Our Incomes: May we have a head to earn and hearts to spend.

Forbearance: May we have keen wit, but never make a sword of our tongues to wound the reputation of others.

Wit: A cheap and nasty commodity when uttered at the expense of modesty and courtesy.

Cheerfulness and Fortitude: May we never give way to melancholy, but always be merry at the right places.

Generosity: May we all be as charitable and indulgent as the Khan of Tartary, who, when he has dined on milk and horseflesh, makes proclamation that all the kings and emperors of earth have now his gracious permission to dine.

Economy: The daughter of Prudence, the sister of Temperance, and the parent of Independence.

Fidelity and Forgiveness: May our injuries be written in sand and our gratitude for benefits in rock.

A Good Memory: May it always be used as a store-house and never as a lumber-room.

A Health to Our Dearest: May their purses always be heavy and their hearts always be light.

The Noblest Qualities: Charity without ostentation and religion without bigotry.

Discernment of Character: May Flattery never be permitted to sit in the parlor while Plain and Kindly Dealing is kicked out into the woodshed.

False Friends: May we never have friends who, like shadows, keep close to us in the sunshine only to desert us in a cloudy day or in the night.

A Competence: May we never want bread to make a toast or a good cook to prepare it.

The Man we Love: He who thinks most good and speaks least ill of his neighbors.

Human Nature as the Best Study: He who is learned in books alone may know how some things ought to be, but he who reads men learns how things are.

Metaphysics the Noblest of the Sciences: "When a mon wha' kens naething aboot ony subject, takes a subject that nae mon kens onything aboot and explains it to anither mon still more ignorant—that's Metaphysics."

The Deeds of Men: The best interpreters of their motives.

Love and Affection: The necessary basis for a happy life.

Charity: A mantle of heavenly weaving used to cover the faults of our neighbors.

Charitable Allowances: May our eyes be no keener when we look upon the faults of others than when we survey our own.

Cheerful Courage:
" May this be our maxim whene'er we are twirled,
A fig for the cares of this whirl-a-gig world."

A Golden Maxim: To err is human, to forgive divine.

Prudence in Speech: The imprudent man reflects upon what he has said, the wise man upon what he is going to say.

Thought and Speech: It is much safer to always think what we say than always to say what we think.

Everybody: May no one now feel that he has been omitted.

Fame: The great undertaker who pays little attention to the living but makes no end of parade over the dead.

The Chatterbox: May he give us a few brilliant flashes of silence.

Discretion in Speech: May we always remember the manner, the place, and the time.

A Happy Future: May the best day we have seen be worse than the worst that is to come.

HUMOROUS TOASTS.

To a Fat Friend: May your shadow never grow less.

May every Hair of your head be as a shining Candle to light you to glory.

Long Life to our Friends: May the chicken never be hatched that will scratch on their graves.

Confusion to the Early Bird: May it and the worm both be picked up.

The Nimble Penny: May it soon grow into a dime and then swell into a dollar.

To a Sovereign: not the kind that sits on a throne, but the one that lies in our pocket.

Our Land: May we live happy in it and never be sent out of it for our country's good.

Three Great Commanders: May we always be under the orders of General Peace, General Plenty and General Prosperity.

The Three Best Doctors: May Doctor Quiet, Doctor Diet, and Doctor Good Conscience ever keep us well.

The Health of that wise and good Man who kept a Dog and yet did his own barking!

Here's to the health of ———: The old bird that was not caught with chaff.

The Health of those we Love the best: Our noble selves.

MISCELLANEOUS ADDRESSES

Every year new occasions arise that point to a new order of celebrations. Until recently there were no centennial celebrations. Once inaugurated these suggested semi-centennial and quarter-century ones, and as the country advanced in years there came the bi-centennial and ter-centennial. And the attention of the civilized globe was called to our fourth-centennial by the unrivalled and wonderful display at the World's Exhibition in Chicago.

In this chapter are given outlines of a miscellaneous character, some original and some selected.

OUTLINE OF CHAUNCEY M. DEPEW'S ADDRESS AT THE
CENTENNIAL OF CAPTURE OF ANDRÉ

This is a good model for the semi-centennial or centennial of any noted event.

Being in the open air the speaker referred to the grand scenery, almost the same as one hundred years before.

Effect on the nation's heart of such Revolutionary commemorations.

87

Small events influence the currents of history. Thermopylæ and its 300; *the three plain farmers who preserved American liberty.*

The orator then sketched compactly but vividly the critical situation of 1780, and tells at length the story of Arnold's treason, its frustration by the capture of André and his pathetic fate. This "one romance of the Revolution" is a thrilling tale, and all adornment is given to it. The account of the struggle to save André's life gives the interest of controversy, as does the defense of Washington's course. The anecdote and the illustrative parallel are both supplied by the case of Captain Nathan Hale, executed by the English as an American spy. The address closes with a fitting tribute to André's three captors, whose modest monument marked the spot, and a very effective quotation of William of Orange's heroic oath at his coronation, "I will maintain."

OUTLINE OF SPEECH BY GOVERNOR FORAKER AT THE DEDICATION OF OHIO'S MONUMENT TO THE ANDREWS RAIDERS, AT CHATTANOOGA

Why this monument and this dedication. The story of the raid, the suffering of the raiders, and heroism of those who died.

The controversial part covered two points—the

military value of the raid, and the manner in which the raiders had been treated by the enemy while prisoners.

The illustrative setting was the historic background of Chattanooga and the contrasts of war and peace.

OUTLINE OF ADDRESS BY CHAUNCEY M. DEPEW AT DINNER ON THE 70TH BIRTHDAY OF JOHN JAY

Not on the programme—pleasantry with Mr. Choate (President) about his railroad fees. Mr. Choate wants it made the rule for all ex-presidents of the club to have a dinner on their 70th birthday. This will help them to live at least that long, as Gladstone and Bismarck, when they had an object, have lived on in spite of the doctors!

Depew, a native of the same county as three generations of Jays. Services of the Revolutionary Jay.

The Anecdote.—General Sherman yesterday told a beautiful young girl—Generals always interested in beautiful young girls—that he would be willing to throw away all he was doing or had done to start at her time of life again. But the nation could not permit that, nor could it in the case of John Jay— closing words of tribute and esteem to the guest of the evening.

OUTLINE OF ADDRESS BY CHAUNCEY M. DEPEW AT
THE RECEPTION TO HENRY M. STANLEY
BY THE LOTUS CLUB

The speaker jests about his own locks whitened by the cares of railroading, and the raven hair of the reporters—where do they get their dye?

Stanley's lecture fee, $250.—Lotus Club gets one for only the price of a dinner!

Stanley a great artist in his descriptions as well as a great traveler.

Americans a nation of travelers.—This makes railroads prosperous! What some reporters have done.

The motive makes heroism.—Livingstone the missionary—his rescue by Stanley.

The civilized Africa of the future with Stanley for its Columbus.

SPEECHES AT A DINNER GIVEN TO THE RELIGIOUS PRESS

Toast.—"The Religious Press and Literature."

First, what are sound views of literature; second, what is a religious paper? The speaker used two illustrations bound in one. A great book is the Nilometer which measures intellectual life as the original Nilometer measured the life and fertility of the land of Egypt. A description of the rise of the Nile and of the *Divine Comedy* of Dante, as such a measurer of the life of the Middle Ages, made up the speech.

Toast.—" Religious Press and Questions of the Day."

Eternity begins *here*. The paper must show on which side of any question the right lies. It should go even further than this. It should cover a wider range of topics and aim to secure the attention of the general public to the questions it discusses and so entitle it to circulate more widely.

Toast.—" Should Religious Papers Make Money?"

If I may make the paying papers, anybody may make the others. Money losing—soon comes, *hic jacet:* Money making proves usefulness and renders the issue of a paper possible. Letter from the oldest editor of New York in which he says the editor is under life sentence to hard labor.

Toast.—" The Religious Paper and Scholarship."

He laments that he has no letter from an editor to read (like the last speaker), and tells a story of a Methodist, on request, praying for rain; and when a terrible storm came, the man who asked, was heard to murmur: " How these Methodists do exaggerate." This was to show the excellence of the dinner. Two other stories were used by the speaker, about the length and discursiveness of his talk. The people need and will read deep, accurate, and scholarly productions. There ought to be a general paper for such. Something has been done in that direction by two religious papers.

The speaker treated his topic by giving a semi-humorous review of the preceding speeches. He showed how denominational traits affected each item in the work of the paper. He did not make just the kind of a paper *he* liked best, for some people were of the same taste as Artemus Ward, who always ordered *hash* at a restaurant, because he then knew what he was getting! The speaker also referred ironically to the mistaken idea that church papers could not pay, and gave striking instances to the contrary. He concluded that denominational papers may be as successful in their line as those purely undenominational and independent.

RESPONSE TO THE TOAST,
"THE NAVY : OUR COUNTRY'S BEST WALL OF DEFENSE"

1. The disasters which different ports of our country have experienced from invading forces during three great wars. No foe now on this continent which we need fear—our enemies, if any, will come by sea.

2. The defense by fortified harbors cannot be relied on, for when one place is defended another may

be attacked, and the coast-line is so great that an un-guarded spot may be found. But our glorious navy will seek the foe at any and every point.

3. Past glory of the Navy. Paul Jones in the Revolutionary War singeing John Bull's beard at his own fireside. 1812. The ships of iron that kept the Confederate States engirdled and forbade outside meddling with domestic troubles.

4. The Navy, by showing the world that we are impregnable, should be the best promoter of a solid peace.

RESPONSE TO THE TOAST,
" GENERAL JACKSON : A DIAMOND IN THE ROUGH,
BUT A DIAMOND "

1. The hero of New Orleans, though rough, was a strong and great man. Stories about him always popular. His indorsing State papers "O. K." when he approved them, and saying that these letters meant " *oll korrect*." The victor and the spoils.

2. His connection with great questions, such as the currency and nullification. Popularity with his own party.

3. Proved to be a great commander by the manner in which he used his very slender resources at the battle of New Orleans—the backwoods riflemen and the breastworks of cotton.

RESPONSE TO THE TOAST,
⋆ THE WORKING MAN: MAY HE LOVE HIS WORK AND HAVE PLENTY OF IT, WITH GOOD WAGES PROMPTLY PAID"

1. For a healthy man a reasonable amount of work is no misfortune, but a blessing. Idleness is a curse, and leads to all kinds of evil. (See story in Anecdote No. 21 at end of this volume—of the tramp who earned seventy-five cents and quit work because he feared that he could not bear the curse of riches! Not many of us have this kind of fear.)

2. Toil with pen and brain as real, and may be as exhausting as with the hand and foot.

3. But to defraud a workman of one cent of his earnings is a peculiarly atrocious crime. How this may be done indirectly. All persons who believe in this toast should deal justly and fairly, and try to hold others to the same rule.

4. The true workman wants work and fair play; not patronage and flattery, but sympathy and friendship.

A NOMINATING SPEECH

The great conventions that nominate candidates for the Presidency of the United States furnish examples on the largest scale of the nominating speech.

But officers of societies of almost any character may be nominated in addresses that are very similar. The following outline of a speech of general character may be easily modified to suit any case in which such help is desired.

Mr. Chairman: It gives me great pleasure to place before you, the name of a candidate who is so well qualified and so fully deserving of this honor, and of every other, that may be conferred upon him, as ———. In giving him your votes, you can make no mistake. [Here state previous offices held, or trusts filled, or other evidences of fitness for the post in view.] In addition, I am happy to state that he represents [here name locality, section, class, or opinion, being careful to adduce only those which will be pleasing to the persons whose votes are sought.] On his behalf, I can promise faithful service, and the prompt discharge of every duty. Others may have as much zeal for the cause: some may have as long a training for the duties of this office; a few may possibly have as legitimate a claim upon any honors or rewards in your gift, but where else can you find such a combination of claims?

The illustrative anecdote will naturally be of the candidate himself, of his popularity, availability, or other good quality, or of some person or element strongly supporting him.

SPEECH ACCEPTING A NOMINATION

1. An honor of which any man must be deeply sensible as well as proud. The importance or high character of the body making the nomination.

2. The degree of surprise felt that the candidate should be preferred to so many worthy competitors. Why the honor is especially prized, and the reasons, if any; why the candidate would have preferred a different selection.

3. The motives which make him willing to bear the burdens entailed by this nomination.

4. The hope of being able to support his competitors for other offices, or other terms of this office.

5. With all his sense of unworthiness, the candidate dares not set up his judgment against that of the honorable body which has named him, for the office of ————, and he therefore bows to their decision and gratefully accepts the [unexpected ?] honor conferred upon him. Should the people—not for his sake, but for the sake of the cause represented—have the intelligence and good judgment [of which there is not a shadow of doubt?] to indorse the nomination, he will exert all the power he possesses, to faithfully fill the position their choice has bestowed upon him.

SPEECH IN A POLITICAL CANVASS

No form of speech is so easy as a political address in a hot campaign. The people know enough of the general argument in advance, to appreciate a strong statement of it, or the addition of new items. They already have much of that interest in the theme that other classes of speakers must first seek to arouse. The tyro makes his feeble beginnings in the sparsely settled portions of the country, but the polished orator is welcomed by large audiences at the centres of population, and wins money, fame, and possibly a high office. Americans have many opportunities of hearing good speeches of this character, and not only become competent judges, but learn to emulate such examples.

1. A bright story, a personal incident, a local " hit," or, best of all, a quick, shrewd caricature of some feature of the opposing party, will gain attention and half win the battle. A speaker was once called upon to make an address after a political opponent had taken his seat. This man at one time strongly indorsed a measure to which his own party was bitterly opposed. The measure was defeated notwithstanding his opposition, and he was obliged to sanction his party's action. The audience being familiar with this, the speaker referred to it by saying ·

7

"Oh! *he* approves, does he! Imagine a mule kicked, cuffed, pounded, and dragged across a road bracing himself at every step, but forced over at last and tied to a post; then imagine *that mule* straightening himself up and saying, 'Thank Heaven, we crossed that road, didn't we?' It was difficult to move the mule, he was obstinate, but it made no difference. My opponent was obstinate too, but what did it avail!"

2. The criticism of our opponents' platform or principles. Their fallacies, mistakes, and misrepresentations.

3. Their history. How they have carried out all their bad and dangerous doctrines, but have slurred over and allowed to drop out of sight their promises of good.

4. The contrast. Plain statement [and there is nothing more effective in a speech than a plain, clear, and condensed statement] of the opposing issues.

5. The man. [The personal element in a canvass nearly always overshadows political doctrine, except when a new party or new measure is rising into prominence.] Our men brilliant, able, safe. Our opponents the opposite. [Public character only should be criticized. Gossip, scandal, slander are abominable, and seldom well received by any audi-

ence. Poison, the assassin's dagger, and the spreading of infamous stories do not belong to honorable warfare.]

SPEECH AFTER A POLITICAL VICTORY. SELECTED

1. We are masters of the field. Completeness of victory [told in military language].

2. Sympathy for the defeated. We will treat their leaders with Good Samaritan generosity, but we invite the rank and file to enlist with us, unless they prefer to go home and pray for better luck next time.

3. Only by joining us can they get a nibble at the spoils. Probably they will, for many of them are men of seven principles—five loaves and two fishes. The " cohesive power of public plunder."

4. We must not be careless after victory, but reorganize, be vigilant, keep our powder dry. The " outs " are hungry, and an enemy will fight terribly for rations. " Brag is a good dog, but Holdfast is a better."

5. Now let us all rejoice over the defeat of a party many of whose members we respect personally, but which, as a whole, we regard as an immense nuisance.

SPEECH AFTER A POLITICAL DEFEAT. SELECTED

My Political Brethren: You seem to be in the dumps! Don't like the figures; wish they were a

cunningly devised fable.   How did it happen?
Big vote and intolerable cheating cooked our goose.
But we are india-rubber and steel springs, and no
amount of hard usage can take the fight out of us.

Let our opponents laugh!   We are not savage
—would not hurt a hair of their heads personally,
but politically will skin them alive next time.   But
we prefer to convert them, and hope they will hear
our speakers as often as possible before the next
election.

A CHAIRMAN'S OR PRESIDENT'S SPEECH

At a public meeting some one interested in the
object for which it has convened calls the assembly
to order.   After securing attention he proposes the
name of some person as chairman or president
When the nomination is seconded he takes the vote
and announces the election.   It will then be in order
for the person chosen to take a position facing the
assembly and to make a brief speech.

"Ladies and Gentlemen: I have no wish to dis
parage your judgment, although I think it might
have been exercised to better advantage by electing
some of the able persons I see before me.   But I
thank you for this honor, which I appreciate the
more highly and accept the more readily because of
my deep interest in the question of ———, which is

now before us. First, however, please nominate a secretary."

When, however, the president or chairman elected is himself a prime mover in the business for which the meeting is called, it will be perfectly proper for him to extend his speech, upon accepting the chair, by stating clearly but briefly the object of the meeting; or, if he prefers, he may ask some one in whose powers of plausible and persuasive statement he has confidence to do this in his place. Formal argument is not advisable in the opening speech; but the best argument consists in giving a compact statement and ample information. In this way the cause may be half won by the chairman's speech or the speech of his proxy.

A GENERAL OUTLINE FOR ALL OCCASIONS

The Introduction. The speaker's modesty or inability, the lateness of the hour, the merit of preceding speeches, the literary treats that are to follow, the character of the dinner, personal allusion to the president or to the audience—*but not all of these in one address.*

The Discussion. Here refer to the toast or theme—be sure to put in a humorous anecdote. Make it as appropriate as possible, but don't fail to bring it in. Get up a short controversy: set up a man of straw if you can find nobody else, and then make an on-slaught upon him; but *be sure he has no friends in the audience!*

Conclusion. A graceful compliment to some one, a reference to an expected speaker, or a word indicating the part of your subject of which you will not treat, or give a *very* quick summary of what you have already said.

ILLUSTRATIVE AND HUMOROUS ANECDOTES

With a number of the following anecdotes a few suggestions are given as to the manner in which they may be used. The habit of thinking how a good story may be brought into an address should be formed, after which these hints will be superfluous. At the outset they may help to form the habit.

1. INDEPENDENCE OF A MONOPOLY

[A good illustration of complete independence. It can be used as a humorous description of a monopoly or as a compliment to a man who has complete control of his own affairs.]

An inquisitive passenger on a railroad recently had the following dialogue:

"Do you use the block system on this road?" inquired the passenger.

"No, sir," replied the conductor; "we have no use for it."

"Do you use the electric or pneumatic signals?"

"No, sir."

" Have you a double track?"

" No."

" We'll, of course, you have a train dispatcher, and run all trains by telegraph?"

" No."

" I see you have no brakeman. How do you flag the rear of your train if you are stopped from any cause between stations?"

" We don't flag.'

"Indeed!   What a way to run a railroad!   A man takes his life in his hand when he rides on it. This is criminally reckless!"

" See here, mister!   If you don't like this railroad you can get off and walk. I am president of this road and its sole owner. I am also board of directors, treasurer, secretary, general manager, superintendent, paymaster, trackmaster, general passenger agent, general freight agent, master mechanic, ticket agent, conductor, brakeman, and boss. This is the Great Western Railroad of Kentucky, six miles long, with termini at Harrodsburg and Harrodsburg Junction. This is the only train on the road of any kind, and ahead of us is the only engine. We never have collisions. The engineer does his own firing, and runs the repair shop and round-house all by himself. He and I run this railway. It keeps us pretty busy, but we've always got time to stop

and eject a sassy passenger. So you want to behave
yourself and go through with us, or you will have
your baggage set off here by the haystack!"

2. EXPLANATION

[To ridicule extravagant explanations that do not
explain—or unreasonable pretensions to antiquity.]

An old Scotch lady, who had no relish for modern church music, was expressing her dislike to the
singing of an anthem in her own church one day,
when a neighbor said: "Why, that is a very old
anthem! David sang that anthem to Saul." To
this the old lady replied: "Weel, weel! I noo for
the first time understan' why Saul threw his javelin
at David when the lad sang for him."

3. RIDING A HOBBY

[To illustrate hobby-riding—very appropriate
where many toasts and speeches run in one line.]

A boy in Buffalo, N. Y., who was asked to write
out what he considered an ideal holiday dinner
menu, evolved the following:

Furst Corse.

Mince pie.

Second Corse.

Pumpkin pie and turkey.

Third Corse.

Lemon pie, turkey, and cranberries.

Fourth Corse.

Custard pie, apple pie, chocolate cake and plum
pudding.

Dessert.

Pie.

4. HOBSON'S CHOICE

[Suitable caricature for any one who tries to
make merit of doing what he cannot help.]

"If my employer does not retract what he said to
me this morning I shall leave his store." "Why,
what did he say?" "He told me to look for another
place."

5. WHEN TO BE SILENT

[A silent guest might tell this to show that he
had found a way to be of greatest service at a banquet.]

Mrs. Penfield—"My husband has found a way by
which he says I am of the greatest help to him in
his literary work."

Mrs. Hillaire—"How nice that must be for you,
my dear! But how are you able to do it?"

Mrs. Penfield—"As soon as I see him at his desk
I go into another room and keep perfectly quiet
until he has finished."

6. Paying for Your Whistle

[Would be a good answer to one who gave a compliment, and tried in that way to shove off a speech
or other duty upon the one complimented.]

McSwatters—" It's very funny."

Mrs. McSwatters—" What is?"

McSwatters—" Why, when the doctor treats me I
always have to pay for it."

7. Goose-Chase

[Would come in well after several had declined to
speak, the goose being the one who finally consents
and tells the story.]

A lady had been looking for a friend for a long
time without success. Finally, she came upon her
in an unexpected way. "Well," she exclaimed,
" I've been on a perfect wild-goose chase all day
long, but, thank goodness, I've found you at last."

8. The Perplexed Sage

[To show that the chairman may safely confide
in his own power to manage such poor material
as the person who tells the story assumes himself
to be.]

"And now what is it?" asked the sage, as the
young man timidly approached. "Pray, tell me,"

asked the youth, " does a woman marry a man because of her confidence in the man, or because of
her confidence in her ability to manage him ?"   For
once the sage had to take the question under ad-
visement.

9. QUICK THOUGHT

[The following illustrates the advantages of a
happy retort, the importance of a felicitous phrase,
or of quick thought and ready speech.   It might be
said that the preceding speaker was as ready as :]

When Napoleon (then a student at Brienne) was
asked how he would supply himself with provisions
in a closely-invested town, he answered, without a
moment's hesitation, " From the enemy," which so
pleased the examiners that they passed him without
further questions.

10. [The Russian General Suvaroff is said to have
promoted one of his sergeants for giving substan-
tially the same answer.]

The Emperor Paul, of Russia, was so provoked by
the awkwardness of an officer on review that he ordered him to resign at once and retire to his
estate.   " But he has no estate," the commander ventured.   " Then give him one !" thundered the despot,
whose word was law, and the man gained more by

his blunders than he could have done by years of the most skillful service.

11. [The anger of an actor took the same turn as that of the Czar.]

Colley Cibber once missed his "cue," and the confusion that followed spoiled the best passage of Betterton, who was manager as well as actor. He rushed behind the scenes in a towering passion, and exclaimed, "Forfeit, Master Colley; you shall be fined for such stupidity!" "It can't be done," said a fellow-actor, "for he gets no salary." "Put him down for ten shillings a week and fine him five!" cried the furious manager.

12. INSIGNIFICANT THINGS

[The need of accuracy, or how insignificant things sometimes change the meaning, is shown by the following.]

A merchant of London wrote his East India factor to send him 2 or 3 apes; but he forgot to write the "r" in "or," and the factor wrote that he had sent 80, and would send the remainder of the 2 0 3 as soon as they could be gathered in.

13. A very well-known writer had a similar experience. He was selling copies of his first literary

venture, and telegraphed to the publisher to send him "three hundred books at once." He answered: "Shall I send them on an emigrant train, or must they go first-class? Had to scour the city over to get them. You must be going into the hotel business on a great scale to need so many Cooks." I was bewildered; but all was explained when a copy of the dispatch showed that the telegraph clerk had mistaken the small " b " for a capital " C."

14. MAKING AN EXCUSE; OR, JOHNNY PEEP

[A guest pleading to be excused from a speech or a song might say that he wanted to be accounted as " Johnny Peep " in the following story which Allan Cunningham tells of Robert Burns.]

Strolling one day in Cumberland the poet lost his friends, and thinking to find them at a certain tavern he popped his head in at the door. Seeing no one there but three strangers, he apologized, and was about to retire, when one of the strangers called out, " Come in, Johnny Peep." This invitation the convivial poet readily accepted, and spent a very pleasant time with his newly-found companions. As the conversation began to flag, it was proposed that each should write a verse, and place it, together with two-and-six pence, under the candlestick, the best poet to take the half-crowns, while the unsuccessful rhymers were to settle the bill among them. According to Cunningham, Burns obtained the stakes by writing:

> " Here am I, Johnny Peep ;
>   I saw three sheep,
>   And these three sheep saw **me.**
>   Half-a-crown apiece
>   Will pay for their fleece,
>   And so Johnny Peep goes **free.**"

15. STERN LOGIC

[Probably this boy would have seen the necessity of avoiding such rich banquets as this.]

" Say, ma, do they play base-ball in heaven ?"

" Why, no, my dear; of course not. Why do you ask ?"

" Huh ! Well, you don't catch me being good and dying young then; that's all."

16. MISTAKEN BREVITY

[" Brevity is the soul of wit;" and calculation and economy are very commendable; but they may be carried to extremes. This may be used when the last speaker has closed a little abruptly.]

This is the message the telegraph messenger

handed a young man from his betrothed "Come down as soon as you can; I am dying. Kate."

Eight hours later he arrived at the summer hotel, to be met on the piazza by Kate herself.

"Why, what did you mean by sending me such a message?" he asked.

"Oh!" she gurgled, "I wanted to say that I was dying to see you, but my ten words ran out, and I had to stop."

17. Charity Begins at Home

Breslau, a celebrated juggler, being at Canterbury with his troupe, met with such bad success that they were almost starved. He repaired to the church wardens, and promised to give a night's takings to the poor if the parish would pay for hiring a room, etc. The charitable bait took, the benefit proved a bumper, and the next morning the church wardens waited upon the wizard to touch the receipts. "I have already disposed of dem," said Breslau; "de profits were for de poor. I have kept my promise, and given de money to my own people, who are de poorest in dis parish!"

"Sir!" exclaimed the church wardens, "this is a trick."

"I know it," replied the conjurer; "I live by my tricks."

18. Charity; or, a Good Word for Every One—even the Devil.

[It is well to feel charitably and kindly at all times, but especially at a dinner party.]

A friend said to a Scotchman who was celebrated for possessing these amiable qualities, " I believe you would actually find something to admire in Satan himself." The canny Scot replied, " Ah ! weel, weel, we must a' admit that auld Nick has great energy and perseverance."

[If the chairman has been very persistent in calling out reluctant speakers, the foregoing would be a good story to turn the laugh upon him.]

19. Ingenious Reason

[The Scotchman referred to in the last anecdote was as ingenious in finding a reason as the boy mentioned in the following :]

" Can you suggest any reason why I should print your poem ?" said the overbearing editor.

The dismal youth looked thoughtful, and then replied :

" You know I always inclose a stamp for the return of rejected manuscript ?"

" Yes."

" Well, if you print it you can keep the stamp."

8

20. Ambiguity of Words

[The equivocal use of words in our language.]

Recently a west-bound train on the Fitchburg (Mass.) Railroad had just left the town of Athol when the conductor noticed among the new passengers a young man of intelligent appearance. He asked for the young man's fare, and the latter handed him a ticket to Miller's Falls and with it a cent. For a moment the conductor suspected a joke, but a look at the passenger's face convinced him to the contrary.

"What is this cent for?" the conductor asked.

"Why, I see," answered the young fellow, "that the ticket isn't good unless it is stamped, and as I don't happen to have a stamp with me I give you the cent instead. You can put it on, can't you?"

The good-natured conductor handed back the coin with a smile, remarking that it was a small matter, and he would see that it was all right.

21. Useless Regret

[Persons who pretend to regret something without making a real effort to better it are hit off by this anecdote.]

A father called his son rather late in the morning, and finding him still abed, indignantly demanded :

"Are you not *ashamed* to be caught asleep this time of day?"

" Yes, father," returned the ingenious youth, " but I'd ruther *be ashamed* than git up."

22. No Happiness in Wealth

[The great advantage of being fully adapted to one's situation and contented with it.]

There are people who cannot hold their heads under the influence of sudden riches. They immediately begin to degenerate. They have become so used to humble circumstances that wealth is a curse. Here is a case:

A tramp, for some mysterious reason, had accepted an offer to work about the place, for which he was to receive his meals, sundry old clothes, and 25 cents a day in cash. For the first two or three days he did very well, and he was paid 50 cents on account. He did not spend the money, but he began to grow listless and sad, and at the end of the week he interviewed his employer.

" You've been very kind to me, sir," he said, " and I want to thank you for what you have done."

" That's all right," was the reply. " I'm glad to be able to help you."

" I know that, sir, and I appreciate it, but I shall have to give it all up sir."

" What's that for?   Don't I pay you enough?"

" Oh! yes, sir; that isn't it.   I have 75 cents left, sir, but I find that money doesn't bring happiness, sir, and I guess I'll resign and go back to the old ways, sir.   Wealth is a curse to some people, sir, and I fancy I belong to that class.   Good-bye, sir."   And he shambled off down the path and struck the highway.

23. Short but Pointed

[Splendid for a speaker called up rather late in the evening—even if he should make a short speech afterward.]

Being nobody in particular, a Mr. Bailey was placed last on the list of the speakers.   The chairman introduced several speakers whose names were not on the list, and the audience were tired out when he said, " Mr. Bailey will now give you his address."

" My address," said Mr. Bailey, rising, " is No. 45 Loughboro Park, Brixton Road, and I wish you all good night."

24. Reasoning in a Circle

[This is very common, as in the case of the heroine of this story.]

The director of a Chicago bank tells how his wife

overdrew her account at the bank one day last month. "I spoke to her about it one evening," said he, "and told her she ought to adjust it at once. A day or two afterward I asked her if she had done what I suggested. 'Oh! yes,' she answered. 'I attended to that matter the very next morning after you spoke about it. I sent the bank my check for the amount I had overdrawn.'"

25. Extreme Economy

[Economy is a great virtue, but it should not be extreme.]

An old lady of Massachusetts was famed in her native township for health and thrift. To an acquaintance who was once congratulating her upon the former she said:

"We be pretty well for old folks, Josiah and me. Josiah hasn't had an ailin' time for fifty years, 'cept last winter. And I ain't never suffered but one day in my life, and that was when I took some of the medicine Josiah had left over, so's how it shouldn't be wasted."

26. Sensible to the Last

[How we commend those who take our standards and help us.]

A story is told of a late Dublin doctor, famous for

his skill and also his great love of money. He had
a constant and profitable patient in an old shop-
keeper in Dame Street. This old lady was terribly
rheumatic and unable to leave her sofa. During the
doctor's visit she kept a £1 note in her hand, which
duly went into Dr. C.'s pocket. One morning he
found her lying dead on the sofa. Sighing deeply,
the doctor approached, and taking her hand in his,
he saw the fingers closed on his fee. "Poor thing,"
he said as he pocketed it, "sensible to the last."

27. FISHING FOR A COMPLIMENT

[Fishing for compliments is sometimes dangerous.]
A well-known Congressman, who was a farmer
before he went into politics, was doing his district
not long ago, and in his rambles he saw a man in a
stumpy patch of ground trying to get a plow through
it. He went over to him, and after a brief salutation
he asked the privilege of making a turn or two with
the plow. The native shook his head doubtfully as
he looked at his visitor's store clothes and general
air of gentleman of elegant leisure, but he let him
take the plow. The Congressman sailed away with
it in fine style, and plowed four or five furrows before
the owner of the field could recover his surprise.
Then he pulled up and handed the handles over to
the original holder.

"By gravy, mister," said the farmer, admiringly, "air you in the aggercultural business?"

"No," laughed the statesman.

"Y'ain't selling plows?"

"No."

"Then what in thunder air you?"

"I'm the member of Congress from this district."

"Air you the man I voted for and that I've been reading about in the papers doin' legislatin' and sich in Washington?"

"Yes."

"Well, by hokey, mister," said the farmer, as he looked with admiration over the recently-plowed furrows, "ef I'd a had any idea that I was votin' fer a waste of sich good farmin' material I'd voted fer the other candidate as shore as shootin'."

28. BEYOND EXPRESSION

[When called on for a speech one may answer the chairman in the words of this lady:]

She was in her room when some people came to call. Her husband received the company, and after awhile said to his daughter, who was playing about the room:

"Go up-stairs and tell your mamma that Mr. and Mrs. Blank have come to call."

The child went, and after a while returned and began to play again.

"Did you tell your mamma that Mr. and Mrs. Blank are here?" asked the father.

"Oh! yes."

"And what did she say?"

The little girl looked up, and after a moment's hesitation, exclaimed:

"She said—well, she said, 'O dear!'"

29. The Toast of the Evening

[The comment upon this incident by the editor is not less amusing than the speech.]

It is not always a pleasant thing to be called upon suddenly to address a public meeting of any sort, as is amusingly illustrated by the following speech at the opening of a free hospital by one who was certainly not born an orator:

"Gentlemen—ahem—I—I—I rise to say—that is, I wish to propose a toast, which I think you'll all say—ahem—I think, at least, that this toast is, as you'll say, the toast of the occasion. Gentlemen, I belong to a good many of these things, and I say, gentlemen, that this hospital requires no patronage — at least, what I mean is, you don't want any recommendation. You've only got to be ill—got to be ill.

"Now, gentlemen, I find by the report" (turning over the leaves in a fidgety way) "that from the year seventeen—no eighteen—no, ah, yes, I'm right—

eighteen hundred and fifty—no, it's a '3'—thirty-six—eighteen hundred and thirty-six, no less than one hundred and ninety-three millions—no! ah!" (to a committeeman at his side) "Eh? oh, yes, thank you—yes—one hundred and ninety-three thousand—two millions—no" (after a close scrutiny at the report) "two hundred and thirty-one—one hundred and ninety-three thousand, two hundred and thirty-one! Gentlemen, I beg to propose—success to this admirable institution!"

To what the large and variously stated figures referred no one in the audience ever felt positive, but all agreed, as he had said they would, that this was the toast of the evening.

30. BEE LINE

[He knew how to escape from more than one kind of fire.]

A soldier on guard in South Carolina during the war was questioned as to his knowledge of his duties

"You know your duty here, do you, sentinel?"

"Yes, sir."

"Well, now, suppose they should open on you with shells and musketry, what would you do?"

"Form a line, sir."

"What! one man form a line?"

"Yes, sir; form a bee-line for camp, sir."

31. Ventriloquism

["Take the good the Gods provide."]

At Raglan Castle, said Mr. Ganthony, the ventrilo-
quist, I gave an entertainment in the open air, and
throwing my voice up into the ivy-covered ruins,
said: "What are you doing there?"

To my amazement a boy answered: "I climbed
up 'ere this mornin' just to see the folk and 'ear the
music; I won't do no harm."

I replied: "Very well, stay there, and don't let
any one see you, do you hear?"

The reply came: "Yes, muster, I 'ear."

This got me thunders of applause. I made up
my mind to risk it, so I bowed, and the boy never
showed himself.

32. A Slight Mistake

[Orders should be strictly obeyed.]

A celebrated German physician, according to a
London paper, was once called upon to treat an aris-
tocratic lady, the sole cause of whose complaint was
high living and lack of exercise. But it would never
have done to tell her so. So his medical advice was:

"Arise at five o clock, take a walk in the park for
one hour, then drink a cup of tea, then walk another
hour, and take a cup of chocolate. Take breakfast
at eight."

Her condition improved visibly, until one fine morning the carriage of the baroness was seen to approach the physician's residence at lightning speed. The patient dashed up to the doctor's house, and on his appearing on the scene she gasped out:

" O doctor! I took the chocolate first!"

" Then drive home as fast as you can," directed the astute disciple of Æsculapius, rapidly writing a prescription, " and take this emetic. The tea must be underneath."

The grateful patient complied. She is still improving.

33. Presence of Mind

[A fine story to illustrate the value (money value) of presence of mind.]

A witty person whom Bismarck was commissioned by the Emperor to decorate with the Iron Cross of the first class, discomfited the Chancellor's attempt to chaff him. " I am authorized," said Bismarck, " to offer you one hundred thalers instead of the cross." " How much is the cross worth?" asked the soldier. " Three thalers." " Very well, then, your highness, I'll take the cross and ninety-seven thalers." Bismarck was so surprised and pleased by the ready shrewdness of the reply that he gave the man both the cross and the money.

34. Joke on a Dude

[A good story for one who has some power of personation, for the dudes get little sympathy.]

A crowded car ran down the other evening. Within was a full-blown, eye-glassed, drab-gaitered dude, apparently satisfied that he was jammed in among an admiring community. On the rear platform a cheery young mechanic was twitting the conductor and occasionally making a remark to a fresh passenger. Everybody took it in good part as a case of inoffensive high spirits, all but the dude, who evinced a strong disgust.

When the young man called out to an old gentleman, "Sit out here, guvinor, on the back piazza," or to another, "Don't crowd there; stay where the breezes blow," the dude looked daggers, and at last, grabbing the conductor's elbow and indicating the young man by a nod of the head, evidently entered a protest. Every one saw it. So did the young man, and he gathered his wits together like a streak to finish that dude. He did it all with an imperturbable good humor and seriousness which would carry conviction to the most doubting.

"Well, I never!" he began, poking his head inside the doorway with an air of comic surprise. "Jes' to see you a-sitting there, dressed up like that. Catch on to them gaiters, will you? Ain't you got the nerve to go up and down Broadway fixed up like that, and your poor father and mother workin' hard at home? Ain't you 'shamed o' yourself, and your father a honest, hard-workin' driver, and your mother a decent, respectable washwoman? Y' ain't no good, or you wouldn't have gev up your place, and I think I'll go look after it myself and put a decent man in it."

He stepped off the car as if bent on doing this at once, and the dude, unable to resist the ridicule of the situation or defend the attack, hastily stepped off after him.

35. NEWSPAPER REPORTER

[Equally good for a missionary meeting or a gathering of newspaper men.]

A young journalist was requested to write something about the Zenana Mission. He assured the readers of the paper that among the many scenes of missionary labor, none had of late attracted more attention than the Zenana Mission, and assuredly none was more deserving of this attention. Comparatively few years had passed since Zenana had been opened up to British trade, but already, owing to the devotion of a handful of men and women, the nature of the inhabitants had been almost entirely

changed. The Zenanese, from being a savage people
had become, in a wonderfully short space of time,
practically civilized; and recent travelers to Zenana
had returned with the most glowing accounts of the
continued progress of the good work in that country
He then branched off into the "laborer-worthy-of-
his-hire" side of this great work, and the question
was aptly asked if the devoted laborers in that re-
mote vineyard were not deserving of support. Were
civilization and Christianity to be snatched from the
Zenanese just when both were within their grasp?
So on for nearly half a column the writer meandered
in the most orthodox style, just as he had done scores
of times before when advocating certain missions.
Some one who found him the next day running his
finger down the letter Z, in the index to the "Handy
Atlas," with a puzzled look upon his face, knew he
had had a letter from the editor.

36. How a Woman Proposed

[A variation of the old and always pleasing theme.]
They were dining off fowl in a restaurant. "You
see," he explained, as he showed her the wishbone,
"you take hold here. Then we must both make a
wish and pull, and when it breaks the one who has
the bigger part of it will have his or her wish
granted." "But I don't know what to wish for," she

protested. "Oh! you can think of something," he said. "No, I can't," she replied; "I can't think of anything I want very much." "Well, I'll wish for you," he exclaimed. "Will you, really?" she asked. "Yes." "Well, then, there's no use fooling with the old wishbone," she interrupted, with a glad smile, "you can have me."

37. Lucky Answer

[Certainly Thompson would be a lawyer, ready for any emergency.]

In times past there was in a certain law school an aged and eccentric professor. "General information" was the old gentleman's hobby. He held it as incontrovertible that if a young lawyer possessed a large fund of miscellaneous knowledge, combined with an equal amount of common sense, he would be successful in life. So every year the professor put on his examination papers a question very far removed from the subject of criminal law. One year it was, "How many kinds of trees are there in the college yard?" the next, "What is the make-up of the present English cabinet?"

Finally the professor thought he had invented the best question of his life. It was, "Name twelve animals that inhabit the polar regions." The professor chuckled as he wrote this down. He was sure he

would " pluck" half the students on that question
and it was beyond a doubt that that opprobrious
young loafer Thompson would fail.   But when the
professor read the examination papers, Thompson,
who had not answered another question, was the
only man who had solved the polar problem.   This
was Thompson's answer: " Six seals and six polar
bears."   Thompson got his degree with distinction.

38. DOUBLE EDUCATION

A young doctor, wishing to make a good impres
sion upon a German farmer, mentioned the fact that
he had received a double education, as it were.   He
had studied homœopathy, and was also a graduate
of a " regular" medical school.   " Oh! dot vas
noding," said the farmer, " I had vonce a calf vot
sucked two cows, and he made nothing but a com·
mon schteer after all."

39. REMNANTS

[This and the preceding have a little spice of ill-
nature, and while enjoyable must be applied carefully.]

Wife—" Such a dream as I had last night, dear!"

Husband—" May I hear about it?"

" Well, yes; I dreamed I was in a great establish

ment where they sold husbands. They were beauties; some in glass cases and marked at fearful prices, and others were sold at less figures. Girls were paying out fortunes, and getting the handsomest men I ever saw. It was wonderful."

"Did you see any like me there, dear?"

"Yes; just as I was leaving I saw a whole lot like you lying on the remnant counter."

40. INDIRECT AND DIRECT

[The following instances show that it is necessary to heed indirect as well as direct meanings.]

Mr. Callon, M. P. for Louth, Ireland, a stanch opponent of the Sunday Closing and Permissive Bill and personally a great benefactor to the Revenue, replying to the Irish Attorney-General, said: "The facts relied on by the learned gentleman are very strange. Now, Mr. Speaker, *I swallow a good deal.* ['Hear, hear,' 'Quite true,' 'Begorra, you can,' and roars of laughter.] I repeat, *I can swallow a great deal* ['Hear, hear,' and fresh volleys of laughter], but I can't swallow that." A few nights before, in a debate which had to do with the Jews, Baron de Worms had just remarked, "*We owe much to the Jews,*" when there came a feeling groan from a well-known member in his back corner, "*We do.*"

41. An Unmarried Man's Wife

At a dinner at Delmonico's, after the bottle had made its tenth round, one of the company proposed this toast: "To the man whose wife was never vixenish to him!" A wag of an old bachelor jumped up and said: "Gentlemen, as I am the only *unmarried* man at this table, I suppose that that toast was intended for me."

42. A Dilemma

"I am no good unless I strike," said the match. "And you lose your head every time you do strike," said the box.

43. Courageous Girl

[The following is a good instance of an elaborate story and a sharp retort.]

It is not always safe to presume upon the timidity or ignorance of folks. The most demure may be the most courageous. A gentleman who attempted to play a practical joke in order to test the courage of a servant, was nonplused in a very unexpected way. Here is his story:

I am very particular about fastening the doors and windows of my house. I do not intend to leave them open at night as an invitation to burglars to enter. You see, I was robbed once in that way last year, and I never mean to be again; so when I go to bed I like to be sure that every door and window is securely fastened.

Last winter my wife engaged a big, strong country girl, and the new-comer was very careless about the doors at night. On two or three occasions I came down-stairs to find a window up or the back door unlocked. I cautioned her, but it did her no good. I therefore determined to frighten her. I got some false whiskers, and one night about eleven o'clock I crept down the back-stairs to the kitchen, where she was. She had turned down the gas, and was in her chair by the fire fast asleep, as I could tell by her breathing, but the moment I struck a match she awoke.

I expected a great yelling and screaming, but nothing of the sort took place. She bounced out of her seat with a "You villain!" on her lips, seized a chair by the back, and before I had made a move she hit me over the head, forcing me to my knees. I tried to get up, tried to explain who I was, but in vain. Before I could get out of the room she struck me again, and it was only after I had tumbled up the back-stairs that she gave the alarm. Then she came up to my room, rapped at the door, and coolly announced:

"Mr. ——, please get up. I've killed a burglar."

44. Moral Suasion

" What are your usual modes of punishment?"
was among the questions submitted to a teacher in a
rural district in Ohio. Her answer was, " I try moral
suasion first, and if that does not work I use capital
punishment."

As it was a neighborhood where moral suasion
had not been a success, and the children were scarce,
the committee took no risks.

45. Cute Boy

The teacher in geography was putting the class
through a few simple tests :

" On which side of the earth is the North Pole?"
she inquired.

" On the north side," came the unanimous answer

" On which side is the South Pole?"

" On the south side?"

" Now, on which side are the most people?"

This was a poser, and nobody answered.   Finally
a very young scholar held up his hand.

" I know," he said, hesitatingly, as if the excess of
his knowledge was too much for him.

" Good for you," said the teacher, encouragingly,
" tell the class on which side the most people are."

" On the outside," piped the youngster, and whatever answer the teacher had in her mind was lost in
the shuffle.

46. PERPLEXED

Bob—" Hello! I'm awfully glad to see you!"
Dick—" I guess there must be some mistake. I
don't owe you anything, and I am not in a condition
to place you in a position to owe me anything!"

47. BEN FRANKLIN'S OYSTERS

Benjamin Franklin was not unlike other boys in
his love for sophomoric phrases. It is related that
one day he told his father that he had swallowed
some acephalus molluscus, which so alarmed him that
he shrieked for help. The mother came in with
warm water, and forced half a gallon down Benjamin's throat with the garden pump, then held him
upside down, the father saying, " If we don't get
those things out of Bennie he'll be poisoned sure."
When Benjamin was allowed to get his breath he explained that the articles referred to were oysters.
His father was so indignant that he whipped him for
an hour for frightening the family. Franklin never
afterward used a word with two syllables when a
monosyllable would do.

48. FAMILY AFFAIRS

"Newlywed seems to find particular delight in parading his little family affairs before the eyes of his acquaintances," "Does he? What are they? Scandals?" "Nop, twins."

49. A BURGLAR'S EXPERIENCE

A New York paper prints this extract from the reminiscences of a retired burglar:

"I think about the most curious man I ever met," said the retired burglar, "I met in a house in eastern Connecticut, and I shouldn't know him, either, if I should meet him again unless I should hear him speak. It was so dark where I met him that I never saw him at all. I had looked around the house down-stairs, and actually hadn't seen a thing worth carrying off. It was the poorest house I ever was in, and it wasn't a bad-looking house on the outside, either. I got up-stairs and groped around a little, and finally turned into a room that was darker than Egypt. I had not gone more than three steps in this room when I heard a man say:

"'Hello, there.'

"'Hello,' says I.

"'Who are you?' says the man; 'burglar?'

"And I said yes; I did do something in that line occasionally.

" 'Miserable business to be in, ain't it?' said the man. His voice came from a bed over in the corner of the room, and I knew he hadn't even sat up.

" And I said, 'Well, I dunno. I got to support my family some way.'

" 'Well, you've just wasted a night here,' says the man. 'Did you see anything down-stairs worth stealing?'

" And I said no, I hadn't.

" 'Well, there's less up-stairs,' says the man; and then I heard him turn over and settle down to go to sleep again. I'd like to have gone over there and kicked him, but I didn't. It was getting late, and I thought, all things considered, that I might just as well let him have his sleep out."

50. HITTING A LAWYER

" Have you had a job to-day, Tim?" inquired a well-known legal gentleman of the equally well-known, jolly, florid-faced old drayman, who, rain or shine, summer or winter, is rarely absent from his post.

" Bedad, I did, sor."

" How many?"

" Only two, sor."

" How much did you get for both?"

" Sivinty cints, sor."

"Seventy cents! How in the world do you ex·
pect to live and keep a horse on seventy cents a
day?"

"Some days I have half a dozen jobs, sor. But
bizness has been dull to-day, sor. On'y the hauling
of a thrunk for a gintilman for forty cints an' a load
av furniture for thirty cints; an' there was the pots
an' the kittles, an' there's no telling phat; a big load,
sor."

"Do you carry big loads of household goods for
thirty cents?"

"She was a poor widdy, sor, an' had no more to
give me. I took all she had, sor; an' bedad, sor, a
lyyer could have done no better nor that, sor."

51. Cutting Short a Prayer

Many a spiritual history is condensed into a minia·
ture in the following:

Two fishermen—Jamie and Sandy—belated and
befogged on a rough water, were in some trepidation
lest they should never get ashore again. At last
Jamie said:

"Sandy, I'm steering, and I think you'd better put
up a bit of a prayer."

Sandy said: "I don't know how."

Jamie said: "If you don't I'll just chuck ye over·
board."

Sandy began: "O Lord, I never asked onything of Ye for fifteen year, and if Ye'll only get us safe back I ll never trouble Ye again."

"Whist, Sandy," said Jamie, "*the boat's touched shore; don't be beholden to onybody.*"

52. Unremitting Kindness

Jerrold was asked if he considered a man kind who remitted no funds to his family when away. "Oh! yes. *Unremitting kindness,*" said he.

53. Amusing Blunder

One of the passengers on board the ill-fated "Metis" at the time of the disaster was an exceedingly nervous man, who, while floating in the water, imagined how his friends would acquaint his wife of his fate. Saved at last, he rushed to the telegraph office and sent this message: "Dear P——, I am saved. *Break it gently to my wife.*"

54. Compliment to a Lady

[How nicely this might fit into a ladies' party.]

Sidney Smith, the cultivated writer and divine, who, when describing his country residence, declared that he lived twelve miles from a lemon, was told by a beautiful girl that a certain pea in his garden

would never come to perfection. "Permit me, then,'
said he, taking her by the hand, "*to lead perfection to
the pea.*"

55. Too Slim

[The great evil of mixing religion and politics are
well set forth in the following incident:]

"Gabe," said the governor to an old colored man
"I understand that you have been ousted from your
position of Sunday-school superintendent."

"Yes, sah, da figured aroun' till da got me out. It
was all a piece of political work, though; and I
doan see why de law of de lan' doan prevent de
Sunday-schools an' churches from takin' up political
matters!"

"How did politics get you out?"

"Yer see, some time ago, when I was a candidate
for justice ob de peace, I gin' a barbecue ter some ob
my frien's. De udder day da brung up de fack an'
ousted me."

"I don't see why the fact that you gave a barbecue
to your friends should have caused any trouble."

"Neider does myse'f, boss; but yer see da said dat
I stole de hogs what I barbecued. De proof wa'n't
good, an' I think dat da done wrong in ackin' upon
sech slim testimony. Da said dat I cotch de hogs in
a corn fiel'. I know dat wan't true, 'case it was a
wheat fiel' whar I cotch 'em."

56. A Fast-day Toast

On one of the fast-days—a cold, bleak one, too—
Father Foley, a popular and genial priest, on his
way from a distant visitation, dropped in to see
Widow O'Brien, who was as jolly as himself, and
equally as fond of the creature comforts, and, what
is better, well able to provide them. As it was about
dinner-time, his reverence thought he would stay
and have a "morsel" with the old dame; but what
was his horror to see served up in good style a pair
of splendid roast ducks!

"Oh! musha, Mistress O'Brien, what have ye
there?" he exclaimed, in well-feigned surprise.

"Ducks, yer riverence."

"Ducks! roast ducks! and this a fast-day of the
holy Church!"

"Wisha! I never thought of that; but why can't
we eat a bit of duck, yer riverence?"

"Why? Because the Council of Trint won't lave
us—that's why."

"Well, well, now, but I'm sorry fur that, fur I can
only give ye a bite of bread and cheese and a glass
of something hot. Would that be any harrum
si-?"

'Harrum! by no manes, woman. Sure we must
ʅ e any way, and bread and cheese is not forbid!"

"Nayther whiskey punch?"

"Nayther that."

"Well, thin, yer riverence, would it be any harrum fur me to give a toast?"

"By no manes, Mrs. O'Brien. Toast away as much as ye like, bedad!"

"Well, thin, *here's to the Council of Trint, fur if it keeps us from atin', it doesn't keep us from drinkin'!*"

57. THE SUN STANDING STILL

James Russell Lowell, when concluding an after-dinner speech in England, made a happy hit by introducing the story of a Methodist preacher at a camp-meeting, of whom he had heard when he was young. He was preaching on Joshua ordering the sun to stand still: "My hearers," he said, "there are three motions of the sun; the first is the straight-forward or direct motion of the sun, the second is the retrograde or backward motion of the sun, and the third is the motion mentioned in our text—'the sun stood still.' Now, gentlemen, I do not know whether you see the application of that story to after-dinner oratory. I hope you do. The after-dinner orator at first begins and goes straight forward—that is the straightforward motion of the sun next he goes back and begins to repeat himself a little, and that is the retrograde or backward

motion of the sun; and at last he has the good sense
to bring himself to an end, and that is the motion
mentioned in our text of the sun standing still."

58. Neutralizing Poison

Col. John H. George, a New Hampshire barrister,
tells a good story on himself. Meeting an old farmer
recently whom he had known in his youth, the old
fellow congratulated the Colonel on his youthful appearance.

"How is it you've managed to keep so fresh and
good-looking all these years?" quoth he.

"Well, said George, "I'll tell you. I've always
drank new rum and voted the Democratic ticket."

"Oh! yes," said the old man, "*I see how it is; one
pizen neutralizes the other!*"

59. General Butler and the Spoons

While General Butler was delivering a speech in
Boston during an exciting political campaign, one of
his hearers cried out: "How about the spoons,
Ben?" Benjamin's good eye twinkled merrily as he
looked bashfully at the audience, and said: "Now,
don't mention that, please. *I was a Republican when
I stole those spoons.*"

60. Making Most of One's Capital

[One should always make the most of his capital, as this orator did.]

"Fellow-citizens, my competitor has told you of the services he rendered in the late war. I will follow his example, and I shall tell you of mine. He basely insinuates that I was deaf to the voice of honor in that crisis. The truth is, I acted a humble part in that memorable contest. When the tocsin of war summoned the chivalry of the country to rally to the defense of the nation, I, fellow-citizens, animated by that patriotic spirit that glows in every American's bosom, hired a substitute for that war, and the bones of that man, fellow-citizens, now lie bleaching in the valley of the Shenandoah!"

61. Meeting Half-Way

[But the following man could get even more out of an unpromising situation.]

"Now, I want to know," said a man whose veracity had been questioned by an angry acquaintance, "just why you call me a liar. Be frank, sir; for frankness is a golden-trimmed virtue. Just as a friend, now, tell me why you called me a liar."

"Called you a liar because you are a liar," the acquaintance replied.

"That's what I call frankness. Why, sir, if this rule were adopted over half of the difficulties would be settled without trouble, and in our case there would have been trouble but for our willingness to meet each other half-way."

62. Unfortunate Mistake

Judge ——, who is now a very able Judge of the Supreme Court of one of the great States of this Union, when he first "came to the bar," was a very blundering speaker. On one occasion, when he was trying a case of replevin, involving the right of property to a lot of hogs, he addressed the jury as follows:

"Gentlemen of the jury, there were just twenty-four hogs in that drove—just twenty-four, gentlemen —*exactly twice as many as there are in that jury-box!*" The effect can be imagined.

63. Taken at His Word

A pretentious person said to the leading man of a country village, "How would a lecture by me on Mount Vesuvius suit the inhabitants of your village?" "Very well, sir; very well, indeed," he answered; "a lecture by you on Mount Vesuvius would suit them a great deal better than a lecture by you in this village."

64. Bragging Veterans

In warning veterans against exaggerating, a gentleman at a Washington banquet related the following anecdote of a Revolutionary veteran, who, having outlived nearly all his comrades, and being in no danger of contradiction, rehearsed his experience thuswise: "In that fearful day at Monmouth, although entitled to a horse, I fought on foot. With each blow I severed an Englishman's head from his body, until a huge pile of heads lay around me, great pools of blood on either side, and my shoes were so full of the same dreadful fluid that my feet slipped beneath me. Just then I felt a touch upon my shoulder, and, looking up, who should I behold but the great and good Washington himself! Never shall I forget the majesty and dignity of his presence, as, pressing his hand upon me, he said, 'My young friend, restrain yourself, and for heaven's sake do not make a slaughter-house of yourself.'"

65. Exchanging Minds

Heinrich Heine, the German poet, apologizing for feeling dull after a visit from a professor said: "I am afraid you find me very stupid. The fact is, Dr. —— called upon me this morning, and *we exchanged our minds.*"

66. Buying a Lawyer

[The willingness to pay full value for an article is a trait of character always appreciated.]

Lawyer B—— called at the office of Counselor F——, who has had considerable practice in bankruptcy, and said: "See here, F——, I want to know what the practice is in such and such a case in bankruptcy."

F——, straightening himself up and looking as wise as possible, replied: "Well, Mr. B——, I generally get paid for telling what I know."

B—— put his hand into his pocket, drew forth half a dollar, handed it to F——, and said: "Here, tell me *all* you know, and *give me the change.*"

67. Would Not Save It

In the old town of W——, in the Pine-tree State, lived one of those unfortunate lords of creation who had, in not a very long life, put on mourning for three departed wives. But time assuages heart-wounds, as well as those of the flesh. In due time a fourth was inaugurated mistress of his heart and house. He was a very prudent man, and suffered nothing to be wasted. When the new mistress was putting things in order, while cleaning up the attic she came across a long piece of board, and was about

10

launching it out of the window, when little Sadie interposed, and said: "Oh! don't, mamma! *that is the board papa lays out his wives on, and he wants to save it!*" Nevertheless, *out it went.*

68. WIDOW OUTWITTED

In a Western village a charming, well-preserved widow had been courted and won by a physician. She had children. The wedding-day was approaching, and it was time the children should know they were to have a new father. Calling one of them to her, she said: "Georgie, I am going to do something before long that I would like to talk about with you."

"Well, ma, what is it!"

"I am intending to marry Dr. Jones in a few days, and—"

"Bully for you, ma! *Does Dr. Jones know it?*"

Ma caught her breath, but failed to articulate a response.

69. TOO KIND

[Where can we find a more touching manifestation of mutual benevolence than the following.]

In New Jersey reside two gentlemen, near neighbors and bosom friends, one a clergyman, Dr. B——, the other a "gentleman of means" named Wilson. Both were passionately fond of music, and the latter

devoted many of his leisure hours to the study of
the violin. One fine afternoon our clerical friend
was in his study, deeply engaged in writing, when
there came along one of those good-for-nothing little
Italian players, who planted himself under his study
window, and, much to his annoyance, commenced
scraping away on a squeaky fiddle. After trying
in vain for about fifteen minutes to collect his scat-
tered thoughts, the Doctor descended to the piazza
in front of the house, and said to the boy:

"Look here, sonny, you go over and play awhile
for Mr. Wilson. Here is ten cents. He lives in that
big white house over yonder. He plays the violin,
and likes music better than I do."

"Well," said the boy, taking the "stamp," "*I
would, but he just gave me ten cents to come over and
play for you!*"

70. Not Fooled Twice

San Francisco boasts of a saloon called the Bank
Exchange, where the finest wines and liquors are
dispensed at twenty-five cents a glass, with lunches
thrown in free. A plain-looking person went in one
morning and called for a brandy cocktail, and wanted
it *strong*. Mr. Parker, as is usual with him, was very
considerate, and mixed the drink in his best style,
setting it down for his customer. After the cocktail

had disappeared the man leaned over the bar and said that he had no change about him then, but would have soon, when he would pay for the drink. Parker politely remarked that he should have mentioned the fact before he got the drink; when his customer remarked: "I tried that on yesterday morning with one of your men, but he would not let me have the whiskey, so you could not play that dodge on me again!" This was too good for Parker, and he told the customer he was welcome to his drink, and was entitled to his hat in the bargain, if he wanted it.

71. Biting Sarcasm

Standing on the steps at the entrance to one of the grand hotels at Saratoga, a young gentleman, in whom the "dude" species was strongly developed, had been listening with eager attention to the bright things which fell from the lips of the well-known wit and orator, Emory A. Storrs.

At last our exquisite exclaimed: "Er—Mr. Storrs, —I—er—wish, oh! how I—er—*wish!* that I had your—er—cheek."

Mr. Storrs instantly annihilated him with: "It is a most fortunate dispensation of Providence that you have not. For, *with my cheek and your brains*, you would be kicked down these steps in no time!"

72. INCORRIGIBLE NEIGHBOR

A lady in California had a troublesome neighbor, whose cattle overrun her ranch, causing much damage. The lady bore the annoyance patiently, hoping that some compunction would be felt for the damage inflicted. At last she caught a calf which was making havoc in her garden, and sent it home with a child, saying, " Tell Mrs. A. that the calf has eaten nearly everything in the garden, and I have scarcely a cabbage left."

The feelings of the injured lady may be imagined when she received this reply : " The cabbage nearly all eaten ! Well, I must get over and borrow some before it is all gone !"

73. DISGUSTED OFFICER

Some years since a party of Indians drove off all the live-stock at Fort Lancaster. A few days afterward Captain —— was passing through the post, and stopped a couple of days for rest. While there an enthusiastic officer took him out to show him the trail of the bad Indians, how they came, which way they went, etc. After following the trail for some distance the Captain turned to his guide and exclaimed: " Look here; if you want to find any Indians, you can find them ; *I haven't lost any,* and am going back to camp."

74. IRATE PRISONER

A man arrested for stealing chickens was brought to trial. The case was given to the jury, who brought him in guilty, and the judge sentenced him to three months' imprisonment. The jailer was a jovial man, fond of a *smile*, and feeling particularly good on that particular day, considered himself insulted when the prisoner looking around his cell told him it was dirty, and not fit for a hog to be put in. One word brought on another, till finally the jailer told the prisoner if he did not behave himself he would put him out. To which the prisoner replied: "I will give you to understand, sir, I have as good a right here as you have!"

75. TRUTHFUL PRISONER

The eccentric old King of Prussia, father of Frederick the Great, while visiting the Potsdam prison, was much interested in the professions of innocence the prisoners made. Some blamed their conviction on the prejudice of judges; others, upon the perjury of witnesses or the tricks of bad companions. At length he accosted a sturdy, closely-fettered prisoner with the remark, " I suppose you are innocent, too."

" No, your Majesty," was the unexpected response, " I am guilty, and richly deserve all I get."

"Here, you turnkey," thundered the monarch, come and turn out this rascal, quick, before he corrupts this fine lot of innocent and abused people that you have about you."

76. RULING PASSION

There are persons now living in Bennington who remember old Billy B——, of whom it might be said he furnished an example of the "ruling passion strong in death." When very ill, and friends were expecting an early demise, his nephew and a man hired for the occasion had butchered a steer which had been fattened; and when the job was completed the nephew entered the sick-room, where a few friends were assembled, when, to the astonishment of all, the old man opened his eyes, and turning his head slightly, said, in a full voice, drawing out the words:

"What have you been doing?"

"Killing the steer," was the reply.

"What did you do with the hide?"

"Left it in the barn; going to sell it by-and-by."

"Let the boys drag it around the yard a couple of times; it will make it weigh heavier."

And the good old man was gathered unto his fathers.

77. Bad Speculation

[This is told of bears, rattlesnakes, etc., as well as Indians.]

At a recent festive occasion a gentleman who was making a few remarks was repeatedly interrupted by another one of the company. He bore it patiently at first, but finally said that it reminded him of a story he had heard. He said that a man, whom business had called away a short distance from his home in the city, thought he would pay his way back again by purchasing a number of hogs and driving them home. He did so, but when he and the hogs arrived at their destination the market for the latter had fallen considerably in price, and the hogs had also lost weight on the journey. It was remarked to him that he had made rather a bad speculation. "Yes—well, yes," he answered reflectively. "Yes—but then, you see, *I had their company all the way!*"

78. Satisfied with His Situation

[The following may not be strictly true, but it well illustrates that there is always a lower depth in misfortune, and—that Western roads are often somewhat muddy.]

Some years ago, when riding along one of the almost impassable roads in the far West, I observed a dark-looking object lying in the middle of the road, and my natural curiosity impelled me to dismount and examine it. It proved to be a hat, somewhat muddy and dilapidated, but emphatically a hat. On lifting it up, to my surprise I found that it covered a head—a human head—which protruded sufficiently out of the mud to be recognizable as such. I ventured to address the evidently wide-awake head, and remarked that it seemed to be in a pretty bad sort of a fix.

"Wa'al, yes!" the lips replied; "you're about right thar, stranger; *but then I ain't anyway near as bad off as the horse that's under me!*"

79. A GOOD WORD FOR THE DEVIL

A conference preacher one day went into the house of a Wesleyan Reformer, and saw the portraits of three expelled ministers suspended from the walls.

"What!" said he, "have you got them hanging there?"

"Oh! yes," was the answer; "they are there."

"Ah! well; but one is wanted to complete the set."

"Pray, who is that?"

"Why, the devil, to be sure."

"Ah!" said the Reformer, "but he is not yet expelled from the Conference."

80. Marrying a Widow

In Cadiz, Ohio, a preacher was summoned to the hotel to make an expectant couple one. In the course of the preliminary inquiries the groom was asked if he had been married before, and admitted that he had been—three times. "And is this lady a widow," was also asked, but he responded promptly and emphatically, " No, sir; *I never marry widows.*"

81. A Good Sale

Several years ago there resided in Saratoga County a lawyer of considerable ability and reputation, but of no great culture, who had an unusually fine taste in paintings and engravings—the only evidence of refinement he ever exhibited. A clergyman of the village in which he lived, knowing his fondness for such things, introduced to him an agent of a publishing house in the city who was issuing a pictorial Bible in numbers. The specimen of the style of work exhibited to the lawyer was a very beautiful one, and he readily put down his name for a copy. But in the progress of the publication the character of the engravings rapidly deteriorated, much to the disgust of the enlightened lawyer. The picture of Joseph, very indifferently done, provoked him beyond endurance, and seizing several of the numbers he sallied forth to reproach the parson for leading him into such a bad bargain. "Look at these wretched scratches," said he, turning the pages over, "and see how I have been imposed upon! Here is a portrait of Joseph, whom his brethren sold to the Egyptians for twenty pieces of silver; and let me tell you, parson, *if Joseph looked like that it was a mighty good sale!*"

82. Triumphs of Medicine

A priest was called upon by a superstitious parishioner, who asked him to do something for her sick cow. He disclaimed knowing anything about such matters, but could not put her off. She insisted that if he would only say some words over the cow, the animal would surely recover. Worn out with importunity, he seized his book in desperation, walked around the four-legged patient several times, repeating in a sonorous voice the Latin words, which mean, "If you die, you die; and if you live, you live," and rushed off disgusted. But the woman was delighted, and sooth to say the cow quickly recovered.

But in time the good man himself was taken sick, and grew rapidly worse. His throat was terribly swollen, and all medical aid was exhausted. The word passed around the parish that the priest must die. When Bridget heard the peril of her favorite pastor she was inspired by a mighty resolve. She hurried to the sick-room, entered against the protest of the friends who were weeping around, and without a word to any one with her strong hands dragged his reverence's bed to the middle of the floor, and with the exact copy of his very gestures and voice marched around the bed, repeating the sonorous and well-remembered Latin phrase, " If you die, you die; and if you live, you live." The priest fell into a fit of uncontrollable laughter, and in his struggle for breath and self-control the gathering in his throat broke and his life was saved!

Mighty are the triumphs of medicine!

83. Tit for Tat

An old fellow in a neighboring town, who is original in all things, especially in excessive egotism, and who took part in the late war, was one day talking to a crowd of admiring listeners, and boasting of his many bloody exploits, when he was interrupted by the question:

" I say, old Joe, how many of the enemy did you kill during the war?"

" How many did I kill sir? *how many* enemies did I kill? Well, I don't know just 'zactly *how* many; but I know this much—I killed as many o' them *as they did o' me!*"

84. Sleeping on Top

During a homeward trip of the " Henry Chauncey,'
from Aspinwall, the steerage passengers were so
numerous as to make them uncomfortable. As for
sleeping accommodation, it was aptly described by a
Californian, who approached the captain, and said:

"I should like to have a sleeping-berth, if you
please."

"Why, where have you been sleeping these last
two nights since we left?"

"Wa'al, I've been sleeping a-top of a sick man;
but he's better now, and won't stand it no longer!"

85. Sambo and the Lawyer

In a Macon (Ga.) court the other day a lawyer was
cross-examining a negro witness, and was getting
along fairly well until he asked the witness what his
occupation was. "I'se a carpenter, sah." "What
kind of a carpenter?" "They calls me a jackleg
carpenter, sah." "What is a jackleg carpenter?"
" He is a carpenter who is not a first-class carpenter,
sah." "Well, explain fully what you understand
a jackleg carpenter to be," insisted the lawyer.
"Boss, I declare I dunno how ter splain any mo'
'cept to say hit am jes' the same difference 'twixt
you an' a fust-class lawyer."

86. SIXTY-CENT NAP

On board a train in the West an eccentric preacher wanted a sleeping-berth, but had only sixty cents, while the lowest price was a dollar. Naturally he did not get on very fast with the porter; but after wearing out the patience of that functionary in vain efforts to stretch the sixty cents, the conductor was sent for. All proposals to borrow, to pledge an old Waterbury watch, and other financial expedients failed; but the circle was squared when the preacher said, " I'll lie down, and *when I have slept sixty cents worth, you send that bed-shaker to rout me out.*" The procession started for the sleeper amid the hilarity of the passengers, but the tradition is that he slept the whole night through and far into the morning.

87. PREFERRED TO WALK

A great traveler once found himself on the shore of the Sea of Galilee. He was at once beset by boatmen, who wanted to take him out to sail on the waters where Christ had walked. He yielded to their importunities, and returned to the shore in about an hour. But his devout meditations were greatly disturbed when he was told that the charge was $10. With energy he declared that it was robbery, that it was not worth so much to sail all over their little lake, and demanded, "What makes you charge so dreadfully?" "Why," said the innocent boatman, "because dese ese de lake were de Saviour walked on de water." "Walked! walked! did He? Well, if the boatmen of that day charged as you fellows do, I should think He *would* walk."

88. HORACE GREELEY'S JOKE

On one occasion a person, who wished to have a little fun at the expense of his constituency, said in a group where Horace Greeley was standing: "Mr. Greeley and I, gentlemen, are old friends. We have drunk a good deal of brandy and water together." "Yes," said Mr. Greeley, "that is true enough. You drank the brandy, and I drank the water."

89. DOCTORS AND DEADHEADS

Fifty years ago the principal avenue of Detroit had a toll-gate close to the entrance of the Elmwood Cemetery road. As this cemetery had been laid out some time previous to the construction of the plank road, it was arranged that all funeral processions should be allowed to pass along the latter toll-free. One day as a well-known physician stopped to pay his toll, he observed to the gate-keeper:

"Considering the benevolent character of our profession, I think you ought to let physicians pass free of charge."

"No, no, doctor," replied the man; "we can't afford that. You send too many 'deadheads' through here as it is."

The story traveled, and the two words became associated.

90. BOOMING A TOWN

They tell a story of a man who came into Omaha one day, and wanted to trade his farm for some city lots. "All right," replied the real-estate agent, "get into my buggy, and I'll drive you out to see some of the finest residence sites in the world—water, sewers, paved streets, cement sidewalks, electric light, shade trees, and all that sort of thing," and away they drove four or five miles into the country. The real-estate agent expatiated upon the beauty of the surroundings, the value of the improvements made and projected, the convenience of the location, the ease and speed with which people who lived there could reach town, and the certainty of an active demand for such lots in the immediate future. Then, when he was breathless, he turned to his companion, and asked:

"Where's your farm?"

"We passed it coming out here," was the reply "It's about two miles nearer town."

91. ATHLETIC NURSE

Young Wife—" Why, dear, you were the stroke oar at college, weren't you ?"

Young Husband—" Yes, love."

" And a prominent member of the gymnastic class?"

" I was leader."

" And quite a hand at all athletic exercises ?"

" Quite a hand ? My gracious! I was champion walker, the best runner, the head man at lifting heavy weights, and as for carrying—why, I could shoulder a barrel of flour and—"

" Well, love, just please carry the baby for a couple of hours, I'm tired."

92. TOO PREMATURE

[Anything rather premature may be illustrated by the following :]

A spring bird that had taken time by the forelock flew across the lawn near this city one day last week. His probable fate is best described in this pathetic verse, author unknown :

> " The first bird of spring
>   Essayed for to sing ;
> But ere he had uttered a note
>   He fell from the limb,
>   A dead bird was him,
> The music had friz in his throat."

11

93. A Bewildered Irishman

The poet Shelley tells an amusing story of the
influence that language "hard to be understood" ex·
ercises on the vulgar mind. Walking near Covent
Garden, London, he accidentally jostled against an
Irish navvy, who, being in a quarrelsome mood,
seemed inclined to attack the poet. A crowd of
ragged sympathizers began to gather, when Shelley,
calmly facing them, deliberately pronounced:

"I have put my hand into the hamper, I have
looked on the sacred barley, I have eaten out of the
drum. I have drunk and am well pleased. I have
said, 'Knox Ompax,' and it is finished."

The effect was magical, the astonished Irishman
fell back; his friends began to question him. "What
barley?" "Where's the hamper?" "What have you
been drinking?" and Shelley walked away unmo-
lested.

94. Obeying Orders

When General Sickles, after the second battle of
Bull Run, assumed command of a division of the
Army of the Potomac, he gave an elaborate farewell
dinner to the officers of his old Excelsior Brigade.

"Now, boys, we will have a family gathering," he
said to them, as they assembled in his quarters

Pointing to the table, he continued: " Treat it as you would the enemy."

As the feast ended, an Irish officer was discovered by Sickles in the act of stowing away three bottles of champagne in his saddle-bags.

" What are you doing, sir," gasped the astonished General.

" Obeying orders, sir," replied the captain, in a firm voice: " You told us to treat the dinner as we would the enemy, and you know, General, what we can't kill we capture."

95. A Speech from the Rear Platform

An Irish street-car conductor called out shrilly to the passengers standing in the aisle:

" Will thim in front plaze to move up, so that thim behind can take the places of thim in front, an' lave room for thim who are nayther in front nor behind?"

96. A Way Out of It

" What's the matter with you," asked a gentleman of a friend whom he met. " You looked puzzled and worried."

" I am," said the friend. " Maybe you can help me out."

" Well, what is it?"

" I am subject at intervals," said the friend, " to

the wildest craving for beefsteak and onions. **It has**
all the characteristics of a confirmed drunkard's craving for rum. This desire came upon me a few minutes
ago, and I determined to gratify it. Then suddenly I
remembered that I had promised to call this evening
on some ladies, and I must keep that promise.
Yet my stomach is shouting for beefsteak and onions,
and I am wavering between duty and appetite."

"Can't you wait until after the call?" asked the
gentleman, solicitously.

"Never," said the friend, earnestly.

"Can't you postpone the call?"

"Impossible," declared the friend.

"Well," said the gentleman, "I'll tell you what to
do: go to John Chamberlin's café; order your beefsteak and onions, and eat them. When you get your
bill it will be so big that it will *quite take your breath
away.*"

97. The Extent of Science

"And now," said the learned lecturer on geology
who had addressed a small but deeply attentive au
dience at the village hall, "I have tried to make these
problems, abstruse as they may appear, and involving in their solution the best thoughts, the closest
analysis, and the most profound investigations of our
ablest scientific men for many years; I have tried, I

say, to make them seem comparatively simple and easily understood, in the light of modern knowledge. Before I close this lecture I shall be glad to answer any questions that may occur to you as to points that appear to need clearing up or that may have been overlooked."

There was a silence of a few moments, and then an anxious-looking man in the rear of the hall rose up.

" I would take it as a favor," he said, " if you could tell me whether science has produced as yet any reliable and certain cure for warts."

98. WHAT'S IN A NAME?

One of the managers of a home for destitute colored children tells a funny story about the institution. She went out there to see how things were getting along, and found a youngster as black as the inside of a coal mine tied to a bed-post, with his hands behind him.

"What is that boy tied up there for?" she demanded of the attendant.

" For lying, ma'am. He is the worstist, lyingest nigger I ever seen."

"What's his name?

" George Washington, ma'am," was the paralyzing reply.

99. Still Room for Research

"What is this new substance I hear so much about?" asked the eminent scientist's wife.

"What new substance, my dear?"

"The element in the air that has just been detected."

"Oh! that, my dear," he answered, beaming over his spectacles with the good nature of superior wisdom, "is known as argon!"

"Oh!"

"Yes; its discovery is one of the most remarkable triumphs of the age.   It has revolutionized some of the old theories, or at least it will revolutionize them before it gets through."

"What is it?"

"It's—er—a—did you say, what is it?"

"I said that."

"Well—ahem—you see, we haven't as yet discovered much about it except its name."

100. He Was "'Piscopal"

An Episcopal clergyman passing his vacation in Indiana met an old farmer who declared that he was a "'Piscopal."

"To what parish do you belong?" asked the clergyman."

"Don't know nawthin' 'bout enny parish," was the answer.

"Well, then," continued the clergyman, "what diocese do you belong to?"

"They ain't nawthin' like that 'round here," said the farmer.

"Who confirmed you, then?" was the next question.

"Nobody," answered the farmer.

"Then how are you an Episcopalian?" asked the clergyman.

"Well," was the reply, "you see it's this way: Last winter I went down to Arkansas visitin', and while I was there I went to church, and it was called 'Piscopal, and I he'rd them say 'that they left undone the things what they'd oughter done and they had done some things what they oughten done,' and I says to myself, says I: 'That's my fix exac'ly, and ever since I considered myself a 'Piscopalian."

The clergyman shook the old fellow's hand, and laughingly said:

"Now I understand, my friend, why the membership of our church is so large."

101. Johnny's Excuse

A little girl brought a note to her school-teacher one morning, which read as follows. "Dear teacher, please excuse Johnny for not coming to school to-day. He is dead." Johnny was excused.

INDEX OF TOASTS

The Figures Refer to the Page

INDEX OF ANECDOTES

POPULAR HAND-BOOKS

SOME books are designed for entertainment, others for information. ¶ This series combines both features. The information is not only complete and reliable, it is compact and readable. In this busy, bustling age it is required that the information which books contain shall be ready to hand and be presented in the clearest and briefest manner possible. ¶ These volumes are replete with valuable information, compact in form and unequalled in point of merit and cheapness. They are the latest as well as the best books on the subjects of which they treat. No one who wishes to have a fund of general information or who has the desire for self-improvement can afford to be without them. ¶ They are 6 x 4½ inches in size, well printed on good paper, handsomely bound in green cloth, with a heavy paper wrapper to match.

Cloth, each 50 cents

THE PENN PUBLISHING COMPANY
226 S. 11th St., Philadelphia

I

ETIQUETTE
By Agnes H. Morton

There is no passport to good society like good manners. ¶ Even though one possess wealth and intelligence, his success in life may be marred by ignorance of social customs. ¶ A perusal of this book will prevent such blunders. It is a book for everybody, for the social leaders as well as for those less ambitious. ¶ The subject is presented in a bright and interesting manner, and represents the latest vogue.

LETTER WRITING
By Agnes H. Morton

Why do most persons dislike to write letters? Is it not because they cannot say the right thing in the right place? This admirable book not only shows by numerous examples just what kind of letters to write, but by directions and suggestions enables the reader to become an accomplished original letter writer. ¶ There are forms for all kinds of business and social letters, including invitations, acceptances, letters of sympathy, congratulations, and love letters.

QUOTATIONS
By Agnes H. Morton

A clever compilation of pithy quotations, selected from a great variety of sources, and alphabetically arranged according to the sentiment. ¶ In addition to all the popular quotations in current use, it contains many rare bits of prose and verse not generally found in similar collections. ¶ One important feature of the book is found in the characteristic lines from well known authors, in which the familiar sayings are credited to their original sources.

EPITAPHS
By Frederic W. Unger

Even death has its humorous side. ¶ There are said to be "sermons in stones," but when they are tombstones there is many a smile mixed with the moral. ¶ Usually churchyard humor is all the more delightful because it is unconscious, but there are times when it is intentional and none the less amusing. ¶ Of epitaphs, old and new, this book contains the best. It is full of quaint bits of obituary fancy, with a touch of the gruesome here and there for a relish.

PROVERBS
By John H. Bechtel

The genius, wit, and spirit of a nation are discovered in its proverbs, and the condensed wisdom of all ages and all nations is embodied in them. ¶ A good proverb that fits the case is often a convincing argument. ¶ This volume contains a representative collection of proverbs, old and new, and the indexes, topical and alphabetical, enable one to find readily just what he requires.

THINGS WORTH KNOWING
By John H. Bechtel

Can you name the coldest place in the United States or tell what year had 445 days? Do you know how soon the coal fields of the world are likely to be exhausted, or how the speed of a moving train may be told? What should you do first if you got a cinder in your eye, or your neighbor's baby swallowed a pin? This unique, up-to-date book answers thousands of just such interesting and useful questions.

A DICTIONARY OF MYTHOLOGY
By John H. Bechtel

Most of us dislike to look up a mythological subject because of the time required. ¶ This book remedies that difficulty because in it can be found at a glance just what is wanted. ¶ It is comprehensive, convenient, condensed, and the information is presented in such an interesting manner that when once read it will always be remembered. ¶ A distinctive feature of the book is the pronunciation of the proper names, something found in few other works.

SLIPS OF SPEECH
By John H. Bechtel

Who does not make them? The best of us do. ¶ Why not avoid them? Any one inspired with the spirit of self-improvement may readily do so. ¶ No necessity for studying rules of grammar or rhetoric when this book may be had. It teaches both without the study of either. ¶ It is a counsellor, a critic, a companion, and a guide, and is written in a most entertaining and chatty style.

HANDBOOK OF PRONUNCIATION
By John H. Bechtel

What is more disagreeable than a faulty pronunciation? No other defect so clearly shows a lack of culture. ¶ This book contains over 5,000 words on which most of us are apt to trip. ¶ They are here pronounced in the clearest and simplest manner, and according to the best authority ¶ It is more readily consulted than a dictionary, and is just as reliable.

PRACTICAL SYNONYMS
By John H. Bechtel

A new word is a new tool. ❡ This book will not only enlarge your vocabulary, but will show you how to express the exact shade of meaning you have in mind, and will cultivate a more precise habit of thought and speech. ❡ It will be found invaluable to busy journalists, merchants, lawyers, or clergymen, and as an aid to teachers no less than to the boys and girls under their care.

READY MADE SPEECHES
By George Hapgood, Esq.

Pretty much everybody in these latter days, is now and again called upon "to say a few words in public." ❡ Unfortunately, however, but few of us are gifted with the power of ready and graceful speech. ❡ This is a book of carefully planned model speeches to aid those who, without some slight help, must remain silent. ❡ There is a preliminary chapter of general advice to speakers.

AFTER-DINNER STORIES
By John Harrison

The dinner itself may be ever so good, and yet prove a failure if there is no mirth to enliven the company. ❡ Nothing adds so much zest to an occasion of this kind as a good story well told. ❡ Here are hundreds of the latest, best, brightest, and most catchy stories, all of them short and pithy, and so easy to remember that anyone can tell them successfully. ❡ There are also a number of selected toasts suitable to all occasions.

TOASTS
By William Pittenger

Most men dread being called upon to respond to a toast or to make an address. ¶ What would you not give for the ability to be rid of this embarrassment? No need to give much when you can learn the art from this little book. ¶ It will tell you how to do it; not only that, but by example it will show the way. ¶ It is valuable not alone to the novice, but to the experienced speaker, who will gather from it many suggestions.

THE DEBATER'S TREASURY
By William Pittenger

There is no greater ability than the power of skillful and forcible debate, and no accomplishment more readily acquired if the person is properly directed. ¶ In this little volume are directions for organizing and conducting debating societies and practical suggestions for all who desire to discuss questions in public. ¶ There is also a list of over 200 questions for debate, with arguments both affirmative and negative.

PUNCTUATION
By Paul Allardyce

Few persons can punctuate properly; to avoid mistakes many do not punctuate at all. ¶ A perusal of this book will remove all difficulties and make all points clear. ¶ The rules are plainly stated and freely illustrated, thus furnishing a most useful volume. ¶ The author is everywhere recognized as the leading authority upon the subject, and what he has to say is practical, concise, and comprehensive.

6

ORATORY
By Henry Ward Beecher

Few men ever enjoyed a wider experience or achieved a higher reputation in public speaking than Mr. Beecher. ❡ What he had to say on this subject was born of experience, and his own inimitable style was at once both statement and illustration of his theme. ❡ This volume is a unique and masterly treatise on the fundamental principles of true oratory.

CONVERSATION
By J. P. Mahaffy

Some people are accused of talking too much. But no one is ever taken to task for talking too well. ❡ Of all the accomplishments of modern society, that of being an agreeable conversationalist holds first place. Nothing is more delightful or valuable. ❡ To suggest what to say, just how and when to say it, is the general aim of this work, and it succeeds most admirably in its purpose.

**READING
AS A FINE ART**
By Ernest Legouvé

The ability to read aloud well, whether at the fireside or on the public platform, is a fine art. ❡ The directions and suggestions contained in this work of standard authority will go far toward the attainment of this charming accomplishment. ❡ The work is especially recommended to teachers and others interested in the instruction of public school pupils.

SOCIALISM Socialism is "in the air." ¶ References
By Charles H. Olin to the subject are constantly appearing
in newspapers, magazines, and other
publications. ¶ But few persons except the socialists themselves have more than a dim comprehension of what it really
means. ¶ This book gives in a clear and interesting manner
a complete idea of the economic doctrines taught by the best
socialists.

JOURNALISM What is news, how is it obtained, how
By Charles H. Olin handled, and how can one become a
Journalist? ¶ These questions are all
answered in this book, and detailed instructions are given for
obtaining a position and writing up all kinds of "assign-
ments." ¶ It shows what to avoid and what to cultivate,
and contains chapters on book reviewing, dramatic criticism
and proofreading.

VENTRILOQUISM Although always a delightful form
By Charles H. Olin of entertainment, Ventriloquism is
to most of us more or less of a
mystery ¶ It need be so no longer. ¶ This book exposes
the secrets of the art completely, and shows how almost
anyone may learn to "throw the voice" both near and far.
¶ Directions for the construction of automatons are given
as well as good dialogue for their successful operation.
¶ Fully illustrated.

CONUNDRUMS
By Dean Rivers

Conundrums sharpen our wits and lead us to think quickly. ❡ They are also a source of infinite amusement and pleasure, whiling away tedious hours and putting everyone in good humor. ❡ This book contains an excellent collection of over a thousand of the latest, brightest, and most up-to-date conundrums, to which are added many Biblical, poetical, and French conundrums.

MAGIC
By Ellis Stanyon

There is no more delightful form of entertainment than that afforded by the performances of a magician. ❡ Mysterious as these performances appear, they may be very readily learned if carefully explained. ❡ This book embraces full and detailed descriptions of all the well known tricks with coins, handkerchiefs, hats, flowers, and cards, together with a number of novelties not previously produced or explained. ❡ Fully illustrated.

HYPNOTISM
By Edward H. Eldridge, A. M.

There is no more popular or interesting form of entertainment than hypnotic exhibitions, and everyone would like to know how to hypnotize. ❡ By following the simple and concise instructions contained in this complete manual anyone may, with a little practice, readily learn how to exercise this unique and strange power.

WHIST
By Cavendish
Twenty-third Edition

"According to Cavendish" is now almost as familiar an expression as "according to Hoyle." ¶ No whist player, whether a novice or an expert, can afford to be without the aid and support of Cavendish. No household in which the game is played is complete without a copy of this book. ¶ This edition contains all of the matter found in the English publication and at one-fourth the cost.

PARLOR GAMES
By Helen E. Hollister

"What shall we do to amuse ourselves and our friends?" is a question frequently propounded on rainy days and long winter evenings. ¶ This volume most happily answers this question, as it contains a splendid collection of all kinds of games for amusement, entertainment, and instruction. ¶ The games are adapted to both old and young, and all classes will find them both profitable and interesting.

ASTRONOMY:
  The Sun and His Family
By Julia MacNair Wright

Can you tell what causes day and night, seasons and years, tides and eclipses? Why is the sky blue and Mars red? What are meteors and shooting stars? ¶ These and a thousand other questions are answered in a most fascinating way in this highly interesting volume. Few books contain as much valuable material so pleasantly packed in so small a space. ¶ Illustrated.

BOTANY:
The Story of Plant Life
By Julia MacNair Wright

The scientific study of Botany made as interesting as a fairy tale. ¶ It is better reading than such tales, because of the profit. ¶ Each chapter is devoted to the month of the year in which plants of that month are in evidence. Not only is the subject treated with accuracy, but there is given much practical information as to the care and treatment of plants and flowers. ¶ Illustrated.

FLOWERS:
How to Grow Them
By Eben E. Rexford

Every woman loves flowers, but few succeed in growing them. With the help so clearly given in this book no one need fail. ¶ It treats mainly of indoor flowers and plants —those for window gardening; all about their selection, care, soil, air, light, warmth, etc. ¶ The chapter on table decoration alone is worth the price of the book. ¶ While the subject of flowers is quite thoroughly covered, the style used is plain, simple, and free from all technicalities.

DANCING
By Marguerite Wilson

A complete instructor, beginning with the first positions and steps and leading up to the square and round dances. ¶ It contains a full list of calls for all of the square dances, and the appropriate music for each figure, the etiquette of the dances, and 100 figures for the german. ¶ It is unusually well illustrated by a large number of original drawings. ¶ Without doubt the best book on the subject.

ASTROLOGY
By M. M. Macgregor

If you wish to obtain a horoscope of your entire life, or if you would like to know in what business or profession you will best succeed, what friends you should make, whom you should marry, the kind of a person to choose for a business partner, or the time of the month in which to begin an enterprise, you will find these and hundreds of other vital questions solved in this book by the science of Astrology.

PHYSIOGNOMY
By Leila Lomax

How can we judge whether a man may be trusted to handle money for us ? ¶ How can a woman analyze a man who would marry her ? ¶ Partly by words, partly by voice, partly by reputation, but more than all by looks—the shape of the head, the set of the jaw, the line of the mouth, the glance of the eye. ¶ Physiognomy as explained in this book shows clearly how to read character with every point explained by illustrations and photographs.

GRAPHOLOGY:
  How to Read Character
  from Handwriting
  By Clifford Howard

Do you know that every time you write five or six lines you furnish a complete record of your character ? Anyone who understands Graphology can tell by simply examining your handwriting just what sort of a person you are. ¶ There is no method of character reading that is more interesting, more trustworthy, and more valuable than that of Graphology, and it is the aim of this volume to enable anyone to become a master of this most fascinating art.

CURIOUS FACTS
By Clifford Howard

Why do you raise your hat to a lady? and why are you always careful to offer the right hand and not the left? ¶ Is there a good reason for the buttons on the sleeve of your coat? ¶ How did your family name originate? ¶ Is it true that it takes nine tailors to make a man, and if so, why, forsooth? ¶ These and scores of equally interesting questions find answers here. Open it at any page and you will see something you have wanted to know all your life.

PRACTICAL PALMISTRY
By Henry Frith

The hand shows the man, but many who believe in palmistry have found no ready access to its principles. ¶ This little guide to it is complete, trustworthy, and yet simple in arrangement. ¶ With this book and a little practice anyone may read character surely, recall past events, and forecast the future. ¶ Fully illustrated.

CIVICS:
What Every Citizen Should Know
By George Lewis

This book answers a multitude of questions of interest to everyone. ¶ It gives intelligent, concise, and complete information on such topics as the Monroe Doctrine, Behring Sea Controversy, Extradition Treaties, Basis of Taxation, and fully explains the meaning of Habeas Corpus, Free Coinage, Civil Service, Australian Ballot, and a great number of other equally interesting subjects.

LAW, AND HOW TO KEEP OUT OF IT
By Paschal H. Coggins, Esq.

Most legal difficulties arise from ignorance of the minor points of law. ¶ This book furnishes to the busy man and woman knowledge of just such points as are most likely to arise in every-day affairs, and thus protects them against mental worry and financial loss. ¶ Not only is this information liberally given, but every point is so explained and illustrated that the reader will not only understand the law on the subject, but cannot fail to remember it.

CLASSICAL DICTIONARY
By Edward S. Ellis, A. M.

All literature abounds in classical allusions, but many do not understand their meaning. ¶ The force of an argument or the beauty of an illustration is therefore often lost. ¶ To avoid this, everyone should have at hand a complete dictionary such as this. ¶ It contains all the classical allusions worth knowing, and they are so ready of access as to require little or no time in looking up.

PLUTARCH'S LIVES
By Edward S. Ellis, A. M.

Plutarch was the most famous biographer and one of the most delightful essayists who ever lived. ¶ To him we are indebted for an intimate acquaintance with many famous Greeks and Romans who made history and who still live. ¶ This book is a condensed form of the original "Lives." ¶ All the personages likely to be inquired about are mentioned, and what is told of them is just what one most wishes to know.

THE DOG
By John Maxtee

Every dog owner should know how to choose a dog, how to house and feed him, how to exercise and train him, and how to get him back to condition if he is out of sorts. ¶ All the essentials of dog keeping are here, from kennel to show-bench, and from biscuits to flea-bane. ¶ For the one who wants a cheap but expert dog encyclopedia in little space this is the only book.

GOLF
By Horace Hutchinson

Golf, to-day, is a synonym for "outdoors" to thousands of busy people. ¶ This standard book gives a complete history of the game, together with instructions for the selection of implements, and full directions for playing. ¶ Much interesting information relating to celebrated links and famous players is presented. ¶ A convenient glossary, together with the rules and etiquette of the game, is appended.

HEALTH: HOW TO GET AND KEEP IT
By Walter V. Woods, M. D.

What is the use of dumb bells every morning and rigid dieting three times a day when there is an open drain in the cellar? ¶ Why shield the baby from draughts and then feed him on infected milk? ¶ Do you know the things that make for Health?—proper exercise, rest, bathing, eating, ventilation, and good plumbing—these are only a few of them? ¶ This book tells what Health is, what makes it, what hurts it, and how to get and how to keep it.

FIRST AID TO THE INJURED
By F. J. Warwick

Lives can be saved and much suffering prevented by the study of this work. ¶ What to do in all kinds of accidents, as well as in the first stages of illness, with a brief and simple statement of the human anatomy, constitute the chief features of the book. ¶ It is written in a plain and simple way, easily understood, and its value is further increased by its copious illustrations.

NURSING
By S. Virginia Levis

Every household has its serious illnesses, but few families can afford a professional nurse. ¶ This book is the next best thing, better in some respects, as anyone can easily follow its instructions, and when once learned they are always available. ¶ The fullest particulars are given for the care of the sick in all the simple as well as the serious ailments of life.

ELECTRICITY
By George L. Fowler

An interesting and thoroughly reliable presentation of the subject for the amateur or skilled electrician. ¶ If you wish to install an electric door-bell, construct a telephone, wire a house, or understand the workings of a dynamo, this volume will furnish the required information. ¶ A practical book of inestimable value to everyone.

BUSINESS LETTERS

By Calvin O. Althouse

Business letters should be business getters. ❡ An expert here shows by numerous complete examples from real business how to write business letters effectively. ❡ There are letters of information, application, introduction, recommendation, letters to order goods, sell goods, collection letters, and indeed every letter a business man needs. ❡ The book includes also a full list of business forms.

SHAKESPEAREAN QUOTATIONS

By C. S. Rex

On every human experience and emotion the great poet shed the light of his genius. ❡ Here are more than one thousand subjects, arranged alphabetically, and under each is given from one to twenty apt quotations. ❡ It is Shakespeare condensed, in a form for practical and universal use.

PHRENOLOGY

By Chas. H. Olin

Tells how to examine the head and learn how its shape influences character. ❡ With a little study of this fascinating science you can analyze your friends' characters, provide unlimited amusement, give useful advice, and find a way to success for yourself and others. ❡ Fully illustrated.

CHICKENS

By A. T. Johnson

Illustrated. ❡ A book that tells all about Chickens, how to obtain success with artificial and natural incubation, how to combat disease and vermin, how to feed and otherwise care for the growing brood. ❡ It is thoroughly modern and scientific and at the same time unusually readable.

BIBLICAL QUOTATIONS
By John H. Bechtel

The Bible is a storehouse of human wisdom, and this book is the key to it. ¶ Thousands of quotations are here arranged alphabetically by subjects, providing instantly an apt illustration for any phase of experience. ¶ The book makes the Bible useful in business, literature, education, politics, club life, social affairs, and many other fields apart from religion. Fully indexed.

THE HORSE
By C. T. Davies

A compact but complete encyclopædia of horse knowledge. ¶ It tells how to choose a horse and tell his age, how to raise horses, feed, stable, and care for them, train them to saddle and harness, and cure their ailments. ¶ It is based on the latest researches of veterinary science and is fully illustrated. ¶ A book that will save its cost a hundred times over to any horse owner.

HOME GAMES
By George Hapgood, Esq.

A collection of the newest and best ways of amusing people who have come together for a good time. ¶ Games with cards, pencil and paper, charades, action games, games of thought and memory, and many new ideas for "forfeits" are among the novel suggestions in the book. ¶ The entertainments are adapted for both older and younger people, and every game is clearly explained. ¶ A convenient index helps in finding the game needed for any occasion.

For other books by
Modern Vaudeville Press, visit:

www.ModernVaudevillePress.com